JOHN EZRA BIEN

The Real Estate Blueprint

A Beginner's Guide to Understanding Real Estate Investing

First published by John Ezra Bien 2024

Copyright © 2024 by John Ezra Bien

All rights reserved. No part of this publication may be reproduced, stored or transmitted in any form or by any means, electronic, mechanical, photocopying, recording, scanning, or otherwise without written permission from the publisher. It is illegal to copy this book, post it to a website, or distribute it by any other means without permission.

First edition

This book was professionally typeset on Reedsy. Find out more at reedsy.com

Contents

Introduction	1
What is Real Estate Investing?	4
Types of Real Estate Investment Properties	9
Understanding Market Cycles	18
Basic Terminology You Need to Know	25
Setting Your Real Estate Investment Goals	34
Financing Your First Deal	42
The Importance of Credit in Real Estate Investing	50
Understanding Leverage in Real Estate	57
Conducting Market Research	64
Analyzing Potential Properties	70
Rental Property Investing	76
Flipping Houses for Profit	81
Understanding Real Estate Taxes	88
Building a Real Estate Investment Team	95
The Power of Networking in Real Estate	103
Real Estate Investment Trusts (REITs)	110
Risk Management in Real Estate	118
Negotiation Strategies for Real Estate Deals	124
Closing the Deal	131
Managing Your Property	138
Using Technology in Real Estate Investing	145
Scaling Your Real Estate Portfolio	154
Managing Cash Flow and Profits	162

Avoiding Common Real Estate Mistakes	170
Moving Forward and Staying Motivated	178
Conclusion	184
Ending Notes	186

Introduction

Unlocking the Potential of Real Estate Investing

Imagine building a future where your money works for you—where each property you invest in becomes a stepping stone towards financial freedom and long-term wealth. This is the power of real estate investing. For centuries, real estate has been one of the most reliable ways to build wealth, and it continues to be a key asset class for investors around the world. Whether you're new to the concept of real estate or you're looking to refine your strategy, this guide will walk you through the essential steps to get started.

Real estate isn't just about owning a house or commercial space. It's about creating a robust financial strategy that opens doors to new opportunities. The journey might seem overwhelming at first, with countless factors to consider—from selecting the right property to understanding market trends, securing financing, and closing a deal. But here's the exciting part: once you break down the process and understand the fundamentals, real estate investing becomes not just achievable but incredibly rewarding.

The beauty of real estate investing lies in its versatility. You don't need millions of dollars to get started, and you don't have to be a financial expert to succeed. What you need is the right knowledge, tools, and mindset. This guide is designed to give you all of those things. We will cover every essential element, from understanding different property types to navigating financing, conducting market research, and executing your very first deal.

One of the most compelling reasons people turn to real estate is its ability to generate passive income. Imagine owning a property that brings in consistent rental income while it appreciates in value over time. With the right strategy, this could be your reality. But it doesn't stop there. Real estate offers tax benefits, leverage, equity building, and the potential to diversify your portfolio, making it a cornerstone of long-term wealth creation.

However, the road to success in real estate investing is not without its challenges. Whether you're buying your first rental property, flipping houses for profit, or investing in commercial real estate, there are risks to consider. But here's the good news: by arming yourself with the right knowledge, these risks become manageable, and the rewards can be significant.

In this guide, we'll break down complex concepts into easily digestible steps. You'll learn how to identify lucrative property types, navigate financing options, assess market trends, and avoid common pitfalls that can trip up new investors. We'll also share real-world strategies from successful investors that you can apply right away.

INTRODUCTION

Real estate investing isn't just about understanding the numbers—it's about taking action, learning from each experience, and continuously refining your approach. Throughout this journey, we'll help you develop the mindset and confidence needed to move forward, whether you're aiming to acquire a few rental properties or eventually scale into larger commercial deals.

By the end of this guide, you'll not only have the knowledge you need to embark on your real estate journey but also the excitement and motivation to take that first step toward a future of financial independence. The world of real estate is waiting for you—let's dive in and unlock its full potential.

What is Real Estate Investing?

Real estate investing is the practice of purchasing, owning, managing, renting, or selling properties with the goal of earning a return on the investment. The basic premise of real estate investing is to generate income through property appreciation, rental income, or a combination of both. As one of the oldest forms of investing, real estate has proven to be a stable and lucrative way to build wealth, and it remains a popular choice for many investors worldwide.

Why Invest in Real Estate?

Real estate has long been regarded as a secure way to grow wealth for several reasons. One of the key attractions is that it provides the opportunity for both capital appreciation and income generation. Capital appreciation refers to the increase in the property's value over time, which can result in significant profits when the property is sold. On the other hand, rental income offers a more consistent cash flow stream, especially when properties are rented to tenants.

Additionally, real estate provides an opportunity to diversify an investment portfolio. Unlike stocks and bonds, which are often volatile and subject to market fluctuations, real estate tends to be more stable. Even during economic downturns, real estate often retains its value better than other asset classes, making it a favored choice for risk-averse investors.

The Advantages of Real Estate Investing

1. Stable Cash Flow: One of the most attractive aspects of real estate investing is the potential for regular cash flow. Rental properties, for example, can generate monthly income through rent payments, which can help cover property expenses like mortgage payments, taxes, and maintenance. The surplus cash flow can be reinvested to build more wealth.

2. Appreciation: Over time, real estate tends to appreciate in value, particularly in high-demand markets. This increase in value can lead to substantial profits when properties are sold. Real estate values tend to increase due to factors such as population growth, demand for housing, and improvements to the local infrastructure.

3. Tax Benefits: Real estate offers a range of tax advantages, including the ability to deduct mortgage interest, property taxes, and operating expenses. Investors can also depreciate the value of their property over time, which can reduce taxable income. These benefits can significantly lower the overall cost of owning real estate.

4. Leverage: One of the most powerful tools in real estate investing is leverage. This means using borrowed capital to increase the potential return on an investment. For example, with a small down payment, investors can control a property worth much more. The ability to borrow money makes real estate investing accessible to many individuals who may not have the capital to purchase properties outright.

5. Tangible Asset: Real estate is a physical, tangible asset. Unlike stocks or bonds, properties provide a sense of security because they are real, solid investments. Investors can see and touch their assets, which offers peace of mind.

The Risks of Real Estate Investing

While real estate can be a highly profitable investment strategy, it does come with certain risks that investors must understand before diving in.

1. Market Fluctuations: Just like any other investment, real estate is subject to market fluctuations. Property values can drop due to economic downturns, changes in local market conditions, or natural disasters. While real estate generally appreciates over the long term, there are periods where the market may experience declines.

2. Illiquidity: Unlike stocks or bonds, real estate is not a liquid

asset. Selling a property can take time, and in some cases, it may be difficult to sell quickly without incurring a loss. This illiquidity means that investors must be prepared to hold their investments for an extended period to realize a return.

3. High Initial Capital: Although leverage can help investors control large properties with a small amount of capital, the initial cost of purchasing real estate is still substantial. Many new investors may struggle with securing financing or may need to rely on high-interest loans or other forms of funding.

4. Property Management: Managing a property can be time-consuming and require expertise, especially if it involves dealing with tenants. Maintenance, repairs, and tenant issues can be costly and burdensome. Many investors choose to hire property managers, which comes at a cost, further reducing the return on investment.

5. Unexpected Expenses: Real estate investments are prone to unexpected expenses, such as major repairs, maintenance costs, or increases in property taxes. These costs can eat into an investor's profit margins, so it's important to have a financial cushion and a solid budget in place.

How to Get Started in Real Estate Investing

To start investing in real estate, you need to establish a clear understanding of the basics. First, consider your financial goals. Are you looking for quick profits through flipping properties, or are you seeking long-term income from rental properties? Once you have defined your goals, research the local market to identify areas with potential for appreciation or rental income. Networking with experienced investors, attending real estate seminars, and learning about different financing options are also crucial steps in getting started.

Real estate investing offers numerous opportunities for wealth creation, but it requires careful planning and a solid understanding of the market. By weighing the advantages and risks, investors can make informed decisions that align with their financial goals. Whether you're seeking steady income, capital appreciation, or both, real estate can be a powerful tool to help you build long-term wealth. As with any investment, success in real estate relies on knowledge, strategy, and persistence.

Types of Real Estate Investment Properties

Real estate investing is not a one-size-fits-all strategy. Different property types offer distinct opportunities and challenges, each appealing to investors with varying financial goals and risk tolerances. In this chapter, we will explore the four main types of real estate investment properties: residential, commercial, industrial, and land. Each property type serves a unique purpose, and understanding these differences is key to making informed investment decisions.

Residential Properties

Residential properties are the most common type of real estate investment and are generally the first choice for new investors. These properties are used primarily for people to live in, and they can range from single-family homes to multi-family buildings like duplexes, triplexes, or apartment complexes.

Benefits of Residential Properties:

1. Stable Demand: People will always need a place to live, which creates a relatively stable demand for rental properties. Whether you're renting out a single-family home or a larger multi-family unit, the market for residential rentals tends to remain strong.

2. Lower Entry Barriers: Residential properties often have lower purchase prices compared to commercial or industrial properties, making them more accessible to investors with limited capital. Additionally, financing options for residential properties, such as government-backed loans or lower down payments, are more abundant.

3. Cash Flow Potential: Residential properties can generate steady rental income, especially in areas with high demand for housing. Investors can also increase cash flow by upgrading the property or raising rent prices as market conditions improve.

4. Appreciation: Over time, residential properties in desirable locations typically appreciate in value. Property values rise as the community improves, attracting more buyers and renters.

Drawbacks of Residential Properties:

1. Tenant Turnover: With residential properties, tenants often move out more frequently compared to commercial or

industrial tenants, leading to potential gaps in rental income.

2. Management Demands: Property management can be demanding. Issues like late rent payments, maintenance requests, or tenant disputes require attention and can become burdensome for investors without property management experience.

Commercial Properties

Commercial real estate includes properties that are used for business purposes. These range from office buildings, retail spaces, medical facilities, to mixed-use developments where both businesses and residents share space. Commercial properties are generally larger in size and higher in cost compared to residential properties.

Benefits of Commercial Properties:

1. Higher Rental Income: Commercial properties typically offer higher rental income due to their larger scale. Retail spaces, office buildings, or shopping centers can generate substantial returns, especially in busy, high-traffic areas.

2. Long-Term Leases: Tenants in commercial properties often sign longer leases, sometimes lasting 5–10 years. This provides stability and predictability in rental income compared to the

shorter-term leases typical of residential properties.

3. Triple Net Leases (NNN): In a triple net lease, the tenant is responsible for paying property taxes, insurance, and maintenance costs, in addition to the rent. This minimizes the financial risk for the property owner and enhances cash flow.

4. Appreciation Potential: Commercial properties often appreciate faster than residential properties, particularly in urban or high-demand commercial zones.

Drawbacks of Commercial Properties:

1. High Initial Investment: Commercial properties typically require a large upfront investment, and financing may be harder to secure compared to residential properties. Higher purchase prices mean higher down payments and closing costs.

2. Market Sensitivity: Commercial real estate can be more sensitive to economic downturns. Retail spaces and office buildings, for instance, may face high vacancy rates during economic recessions when businesses downsize or close.

3. Management Complexity: Managing commercial properties can be more complex than managing residential properties,

especially if the property houses multiple tenants with different needs. This may require specialized property management expertise.

Industrial Properties

Industrial real estate includes warehouses, manufacturing plants, distribution centers, and storage facilities. These properties are used for business purposes related to production, storage, or distribution of goods.

Benefits of Industrial Properties:

1. Long-Term Leases and Stability: Industrial tenants often sign long-term leases (5-10 years), providing stability to property owners. This is particularly true for large distribution centers or warehouses used by companies in industries like logistics or e-commerce.

2. Higher Yields: Industrial properties can provide high rental yields due to the nature of the space and its uses. Warehouses and distribution centers, for example, can command premium rents, especially near transportation hubs or ports.

3. Minimal Tenant Improvements: Unlike office or retail spaces, industrial properties typically require fewer renovations or tenant improvements. This reduces the upfront costs

and maintenance required to keep the property attractive to tenants.

4. Growing Demand: With the rise of e-commerce, the demand for industrial spaces, especially warehouses and fulfillment centers, has grown significantly. This trend shows little sign of slowing down, making industrial properties an appealing investment.

Drawbacks of Industrial Properties:

1. Specialized Market: Industrial properties may not be as liquid or easy to sell as residential or commercial properties. The market for industrial spaces can be more niche, depending on location and the type of business it serves.

2. Maintenance Costs: While industrial properties are generally simpler to manage than commercial or residential properties, they can have substantial maintenance needs, especially in terms of machinery, HVAC systems, and other specialized infrastructure.

3. Economic Sensitivity: Like commercial real estate, industrial properties are sensitive to economic shifts. A downturn in manufacturing or logistics sectors could lead to higher vacancy rates or lower rental income.

Land Investments

Land investments refer to buying undeveloped or vacant land for future development or sale. This can include residential lots, agricultural land, or raw land in areas undergoing expansion or urbanization.

Benefits of Land Investments:

1. Low Maintenance: Unlike residential or commercial properties, raw land requires minimal maintenance. There are no tenants to manage, and the property doesn't require regular upkeep unless the investor decides to develop it.

2. Appreciation Potential: Land tends to appreciate in value as areas develop and infrastructure improves. Buying land in an area poised for growth can lead to significant profits when the land is eventually sold or developed.

3. Flexibility: Land offers a range of possibilities, from holding it for future appreciation to developing it into residential or commercial properties. It can also be used for farming or recreational purposes.

4. Lower Entry Costs: While land in prime locations can be expensive, buying raw or undeveloped land often requires less capital than buying residential or commercial properties, making it more accessible for beginning investors.

Drawbacks of Land Investments:

1. Illiquidity: Land investments are highly illiquid, meaning it can take a long time to sell land and realize a profit. Additionally, there is no income generated from owning land unless it is developed or used for agricultural purposes.

2. Zoning and Development Risks: If you plan to develop the land, zoning laws, environmental regulations, and the cost of infrastructure can make the development process costly and time-consuming.

3. Market Volatility: The land market can be volatile, and it is often more difficult to gauge the future value of land compared to other property types. Speculative land investments can be risky without a clear understanding of the local market trends.

Each type of real estate investment property presents distinct opportunities and challenges. Residential properties offer stability and steady income, commercial properties promise higher returns but require larger investments, industrial properties cater to niche markets with long-term leases, and land offers long-term growth potential with minimal upkeep.

Understanding the different types of properties and their

associated benefits and risks is crucial for making informed investment decisions. Choosing the right property type depends on your investment goals, available capital, and willingness to manage the property. Whether you're just starting or are an experienced investor, knowing the advantages and drawbacks of each property type will help you create a balanced portfolio and navigate the complexities of the real estate market with confidence.

Understanding Market Cycles

Real estate markets are never static. They go through cycles of growth, stagnation, and decline. Understanding these market cycles is critical for making informed investment decisions. Whether you're a seasoned investor or just starting, recognizing the phase the market is in can help you optimize your strategy for maximum returns and minimize potential risks. In this chapter, we'll explore the four primary phases of a real estate cycle: expansion, peak, contraction, and recovery. Each phase has its unique characteristics and impacts on investment opportunities.

The Four Phases of the Real Estate Cycle

Real estate cycles generally follow a predictable pattern, but the timing and duration of each phase can vary based on factors like economic conditions, interest rates, and regional trends. Let's break down each of these phases in more detail:

1. Expansion Phase

The expansion phase, also known as the growth phase, is characterized by increasing demand for real estate, rising property prices, and a generally positive economic outlook. During this phase, the market is flourishing, and investors typically see higher returns.

Key Indicators of the Expansion Phase:

Rising Demand: More people are looking for properties, and both buyers and renters are active in the market. This leads to increased sales and rental prices.

Low Vacancy Rates: With strong demand for both residential and commercial properties, vacancies are low, which helps to drive rental income up.

Increased Construction: Developers build more properties to meet the growing demand, particularly in high-demand areas. This includes residential, commercial, and industrial developments.

Favorable Economic Conditions: Low unemployment, rising incomes, and consumer confidence contribute to an expanding economy, encouraging investment and consumption.

Strategies for Investing in the Expansion Phase:

Buy and Hold: Investors should focus on purchasing properties with the intention of holding them long-term, benefiting from both appreciation and rental income.

Development Projects: Expanding markets are a good time to invest in new development or land development projects.

Leverage Financing: With rising property values and favorable lending conditions, securing financing for new properties or projects is often easier during the expansion phase.

2. Peak Phase

The peak phase marks the highest point of the real estate cycle, where property prices and demand reach their highest levels. During this period, the market is typically at its most optimistic, but it's also the time when a slowdown or downturn could be imminent.

Key Indicators of the Peak Phase:

Soaring Property Prices: Property values are at their highest, and investors might be seeing significant profits. However, these elevated prices can sometimes become unsustainable.

High Construction Activity: Developers are building aggressively to capitalize on the high demand. This can lead to an oversupply of properties if the market is nearing a peak.

Overheated Market: At the peak, the market may start to feel the effects of overheating, where demand begins to outpace the economy's ability to sustain it. Speculative investments become more common.

Rising Interest Rates: Central banks may raise interest rates in response to inflation, which can begin to cool off the economy and slow down the market.

Strategies for Investing at the Peak:

Sell or Take Profits: If you're holding properties purchased during the expansion phase, the peak is a good time to sell and lock in profits before the market shifts.

Diversification: It's wise to diversify your portfolio during this phase. Consider reallocating capital into different property types or other investment assets.

Caution with Leverage: Avoid excessive borrowing during the peak, as rising interest rates and a potential market downturn could make high levels of debt more risky.

3. Contraction Phase

The contraction phase is characterized by a slowdown in the market, marked by decreasing demand and falling property prices. This is the period where the real estate market experiences a downturn, often coinciding with broader economic slowdowns, such as recessions.

Key Indicators of the Contraction Phase:

Declining Demand: Both buyers and renters become more cautious, leading to fewer property sales and rental transactions.

Rising Vacancy Rates: With fewer people looking for homes, commercial spaces, or rental properties, vacancy rates increase, putting downward pressure on rental prices.

Falling Property Prices: Property values typically begin to decline as demand wanes, making it a less favorable time for sellers but an opportunity for buyers with cash on hand.

Increased Foreclosures: As property owners struggle with lower rental incomes and rising interest rates, foreclosures and distressed sales may increase.

Strategies for Investing During the Contraction Phase:

Buy Distressed Properties: The contraction phase can present opportunities to purchase properties at discounted prices, especially distressed properties that can be rehabilitated and sold or rented later on.

Focus on Cash Flow: Rental properties with stable cash flow become especially important during this phase. Tenants still need places to live, so income-producing properties with strong tenants can help insulate you from market fluctuations.

Caution with Development: Avoid risky new construction projects during a contraction, as demand will likely be lower. It's better to focus on properties that are already established or in prime locations.

4. Recovery Phase

The recovery phase marks the turnaround from the contraction phase. While the economy and real estate market are still rebuilding, signs of recovery become more apparent, and the cycle begins to move toward growth again.

Key Indicators of the Recovery Phase:

Stabilizing Prices: After a period of decline, property prices stabilize and start to slowly increase again. Although the market may not yet be fully recovered, it begins to show signs of improvement.

Increased Demand: As the economy strengthens, demand for both residential and commercial properties starts to rise again. However, this demand is usually gradual, not immediate.

Low Interest Rates: Central banks may lower interest rates to stimulate borrowing and investment, which can help spark the recovery of the housing and real estate markets.

Renewed Investor Confidence: As prices stabilize and the economy improves, investor confidence starts to return, leading to a gradual increase in activity in the real estate market.

Strategies for Investing During the Recovery Phase:

Purchase with Long-Term View: The recovery phase is a great time to buy properties at a discounted price before the market enters the expansion phase. Focus on long-term appreciation and growth.

Renovation Projects: Properties that suffered during the contraction phase might offer significant upside if purchased early in the recovery. Renovating and improving these properties can help increase their value.

Invest in Emerging Areas: During the recovery phase, certain neighborhoods or regions may begin to see early signs of revitalization. Investing in these areas early on can result in significant returns as the market continues to improve.

The real estate market is cyclical, and understanding these cycles is essential for investors who want to navigate the market successfully. Each phase—expansion, peak, contraction, and recovery—presents unique opportunities and risks. By recognizing where the market stands and adjusting your investment strategy accordingly, you can increase your chances of success and avoid unnecessary losses.

Being attuned to market cycles allows investors to make smart decisions, whether it's capitalizing on growth during an expansion, securing discounted properties in a contraction, or planning for long-term gains in the recovery phase. By aligning your strategy with the market's natural rhythm, you'll be better positioned to maximize returns over time.

Basic Terminology You Need to Know

Real estate investing comes with its own set of terminology, and for anyone looking to succeed in the field, it's crucial to understand these terms. Whether you're discussing a potential deal with an agent, negotiating with lenders, or evaluating investment properties, being fluent in the language of real estate can make a huge difference. In this chapter, we will introduce and explain essential real estate jargon, including important metrics and concepts that will empower you to navigate the industry with confidence.

1. Return on Investment (ROI)

Return on Investment (ROI) is a key metric that measures the profitability of an investment relative to its cost. It is expressed as a percentage and helps investors evaluate the efficiency of an investment.

Formula:

$$ROI = \frac{\text{Net Profit}}{\text{Investment Cost}} \times 100$$

For example, if you bought a rental property for $100,000 and earned $10,000 in profit after expenses, your ROI would be 10%.

Why It Matters:

A higher ROI indicates a more profitable investment.

ROI helps you compare different investment opportunities to see which one yields the highest returns.

2. Capitalization Rate (Cap Rate)

The Capitalization Rate, or Cap Rate, is a crucial metric for evaluating the potential return on a rental property. It's the ratio of a property's net operating income (NOI) to its current market value or acquisition cost.

Formula:

$$\text{Cap Rate} = \frac{\text{Net Operating Income}}{\text{Property Value}} \times 100$$

For example, if a property generates $30,000 in net income per year and is worth $300,000, the cap rate would be 10%.

Why It Matters:

The Cap Rate helps you compare investment properties of different prices and income levels.

It gives a quick snapshot of potential returns, but it doesn't consider financing, appreciation, or tax implications.

3. Net Operating Income (NOI)

Net Operating Income is the total income generated by a property after deducting all operating expenses (excluding mortgage payments and taxes). NOI is a critical figure when determining a property's value and potential profitability.

Formula:

NOI = Gross Income - Operating Expenses

Operating expenses include things like property management fees, maintenance costs, insurance, and utilities, but exclude financing costs like mortgage payments.

Why It Matters:

NOI is used in determining the Cap Rate, which helps investors assess the potential profitability of a property.

A higher NOI means higher potential returns.

4. Gross Rent Multiplier (GRM)

The Gross Rent Multiplier is a simple way to estimate the value of a rental property based on its rental income. It is calculated by dividing the property price by the gross annual rental income.

Formula:

$$GRM = \frac{\text{Property Price}}{\text{Annual Rental Income}}$$

For example, if a property costs $200,000 and generates $20,000 in annual rent, the GRM would be 10.

Why It Matters:

GRM is a quick way to assess property value and compare different rental properties.

However, it doesn't account for operating expenses, so it's less accurate than NOI or Cap Rate when evaluating profitability.

5. Leverage

Leverage refers to the use of borrowed funds to finance an investment. In real estate, investors often use leverage by taking out a mortgage to buy property, which allows them to control larger assets with a smaller initial investment.

Why It Matters:

Leverage can magnify profits if property values rise, but it also magnifies losses if the property value declines.

Proper use of leverage can increase returns, but it also increases the risk of debt-related issues.

6. Equity

Equity is the difference between the current market value of a property and the amount of money owed on any loans or mortgages. Over time, as you pay down your mortgage and the property appreciates, your equity in the property increases.

Formula:

Equity = Property Value - Mortgage Balance

For example, if your property is worth $300,000 and you owe $150,000, your equity is $150,000.

Why It Matters:

Building equity is one of the primary ways that real estate investors increase their wealth.

Equity can be used to leverage additional investments or to sell for a profit.

7. Cash Flow

Cash Flow refers to the money generated from an investment property after all expenses (including mortgage payments, maintenance, and taxes) have been deducted from rental income. Positive cash flow means you're earning more than you're spending, while negative cash flow means you're losing money.

Formula:

Cash Flow = Rental Income - Expenses

For example, if your property generates $2,000 in monthly rent and your expenses (mortgage, taxes, insurance, etc.) are $1,500, your monthly cash flow would be $500.

Why It Matters:

Positive cash flow is essential for real estate investors who want to maintain long-term profitability.

Consistent cash flow allows investors to cover property expenses, service debt, and generate income.

8. Appreciation

Appreciation refers to the increase in the value of a property over time due to factors such as market demand, improvements to the property, or broader economic growth. Real estate appreciation can result in significant profits when a property is sold for more than its original purchase price.

Why It Matters:

Appreciation is a primary way investors make money from real estate, especially in markets with high demand or ongoing urban development.

It's important to recognize that while appreciation can lead to higher profits, it's also influenced by market cycles and is not always guaranteed.

9. Property Management

Property management involves the operation, control, and oversight of real estate properties. This can include finding and screening tenants, handling maintenance requests, managing finances, and ensuring compliance with laws and regulations.

Why It Matters:

Effective property management is crucial for maintaining cash flow and preserving property value.

Investors who don't want to manage properties themselves often hire property management companies to handle these tasks.

10. Foreclosure

A foreclosure occurs when a property owner fails to make mortgage payments, and the lender seizes the property to recover the unpaid loan balance. Foreclosed properties are often sold at auctions, typically at a price lower than market value.

Why It Matters:

Investors can potentially acquire foreclosed properties at a discount, which may offer high returns if the property is in a desirable location and can be quickly resold or rented.

However, purchasing foreclosures comes with risks, such as legal issues, property damage, or unresolved liens.

11. 1031 Exchange

A 1031 Exchange is a tax-deferral strategy that allows real estate investors to defer capital gains taxes when they sell a property, provided the proceeds are reinvested into a like-kind property within a specified time frame.

Why It Matters:

The 1031 Exchange allows investors to defer taxes, which can lead to more capital being available for reinvestment.

This is an excellent strategy for those looking to build a real estate portfolio without being immediately taxed on the gains from property sales.

BASIC TERMINOLOGY YOU NEED TO KNOW

Understanding real estate terminology is essential for anyone involved in real estate investing. From metrics like ROI and Cap Rate to concepts like leverage and equity, being familiar with these terms allows you to make more informed decisions, communicate effectively with industry professionals, and evaluate investment opportunities with confidence. Whether you're analyzing a potential deal, negotiating financing, or simply discussing investments with fellow investors, mastering real estate jargon will help you stay ahead in the game.

Setting Your Real Estate Investment Goals

Real estate investing can be a highly rewarding venture, but like any business, success is driven by clear goals and a well-defined strategy. Before you begin your real estate journey, it's essential to identify what you hope to achieve. Your investment goals will guide your decisions on what properties to invest in, how much risk you're willing to take, and how long you plan to hold your investments. In this chapter, we'll walk you through the process of setting clear and achievable real estate investment goals based on your financial situation, risk tolerance, and personal aspirations.

1. Understanding Different Investment Objectives

Real estate investments can serve various purposes, depending on the investor's goals. The first step in goal-setting is to understand the different investment objectives that you might have:

a. Cash Flow

If your primary objective is to generate passive income, cash flow should be your main focus. Positive cash flow occurs when the income from rental properties (rent, parking fees, etc.) exceeds your expenses (mortgage, property taxes, maintenance, etc.).

For example, if a property generates $2,000 per month in rent but costs you $1,500 in expenses, your cash flow is $500 per month. Investors focused on cash flow typically prefer rental properties that provide consistent and reliable income.

Why Cash Flow Matters:

It provides regular income that can help cover living expenses or be reinvested.

It offers financial stability and mitigates the risks associated with market fluctuations or property value changes.

b. Long-Term Appreciation

Another common objective is long-term property appreciation. Investors focused on appreciation are less concerned about short-term cash flow and more interested in the long-term growth of property value. These investors may hold onto a property for many years, hoping the property will increase in value over time.

Real estate prices often appreciate due to factors like urban development, increased demand, or improvements in infrastructure. For instance, buying in an emerging neighborhood that is undergoing revitalization can lead to significant appreciation over time.

Why Appreciation Matters:

Investors can sell their property at a higher price in the future for a profit.

Appreciation is often combined with cash flow for long-term wealth-building strategies.

c. Tax Benefits

Real estate investing offers numerous tax advantages that can benefit investors. These include deductions for mortgage interest, property depreciation, repairs, and maintenance. Investors often use these benefits to reduce their taxable income, ultimately increasing their return on investment (ROI).

Why Tax Benefits Matter:

It helps lower your tax liability, effectively increasing your cash flow and ROI.

Tax-deferred strategies, like the 1031 Exchange, can also be used to defer capital gains taxes on property sales.

d. Equity Building

Equity building is another important goal. Equity refers to the ownership value you have in a property after subtracting any outstanding mortgage balances. Every mortgage payment you make increases your equity in the property. Over time, as property values increase and you pay down the loan, your equity grows.

Why Equity Matters:

Building equity allows you to leverage it for future investments or loans.

Increased equity can be used as a source of funding for other investments or a safety net in case of emergencies.

2. Assessing Your Financial Situation

Before you set your real estate investment goals, it's critical to assess your current financial situation. Real estate can require substantial upfront capital, and your financial resources will heavily influence the types of investments you pursue.

a. Personal Net Worth

Start by evaluating your assets and liabilities. Your net worth gives you an overall picture of your financial health and will help you determine how much capital you can invest. While real estate is known for leveraging debt, having a solid foundation in personal finances ensures that you can weather potential risks.

b. Available Cash for Investment

Determine how much liquid cash you have available for down payments, closing costs, and property improvements. Many real estate investors start with a savings fund or use lines of credit. The amount of cash you have on hand can affect your strategy—whether you opt for low-cost, high-leverage properties or choose to invest in higher-value homes with lower debt.

c. Financing Options

Understanding your financing options is another key step. Are you planning to finance your investment with a mortgage, or do you have access to other capital? The type of financing you choose will directly impact your cash flow, ROI, and overall risk profile. For example, higher interest rates can eat into your returns, while using an all-cash strategy might lead to better long-term profitability.

3. Identifying Your Risk Tolerance

Every investment comes with risk, and real estate is no different. It's crucial to define your risk tolerance—how much risk you're willing to accept in pursuit of your goals.

a. Conservative Approach

If you're risk-averse and prefer stability, you might focus on low-risk, long-term investments. This might involve purchasing well-established properties in prime locations that are less likely to experience volatility. Your goals would likely be centered around consistent cash flow and appreciation over time.

b. Moderate Risk Approach

If you're willing to take on a moderate amount of risk, you might explore emerging markets or areas undergoing revitalization. Here, you could balance appreciation with cash flow, knowing there's potential for both short-term and long-term gains.

c. Aggressive Approach

Aggressive investors are open to higher risks and are often willing to invest in properties that may be undervalued or require significant work. They focus on maximizing returns through rehabbing properties (flipping), or they may target high-growth areas with high potential for appreciation. These investors might also consider taking on more debt to increase their leverage.

4. Setting SMART Goals

The most effective way to set investment goals is to make them SMART: Specific, Measurable, Achievable, Relevant, and Time-bound. Here's a breakdown:

a. Specific

Be clear about what you want to achieve. For example, rather than saying "I want to make money through real estate," specify "I want to acquire two rental properties that generate $2,000 in positive cash flow per month."

b. Measurable

Establish metrics to track your progress. For example, how much capital do you need to invest? What return on investment (ROI) are you aiming for? This allows you to monitor your progress and adjust your strategy if necessary.

c. Achievable

Set realistic goals based on your financial resources and risk tolerance. If you have a limited budget, it might not be feasible to buy a commercial property immediately. Instead, you might start with a residential property and gradually expand as you build capital and experience.

d. Relevant

Ensure that your goals align with your overall financial and personal aspirations. If your goal is long-term wealth-building, focusing on properties that provide stable cash flow and appreciate over time may be your best choice.

e. Time-bound

Set deadlines for reaching your goals. For example, you could aim to acquire your first rental property within the next 12 months. Time-bound goals keep you motivated and provide clear milestones to hit.

5. Tracking Your Progress and Adjusting Goals

Once you've set your goals, it's important to track your progress regularly. Review your financial situation, assess your investments, and adjust your strategy if needed. Real estate markets can change, and you may find that your initial goals no longer align with current market conditions or personal circumstances. Flexibility is key to long-term success.

Setting clear, actionable goals is a critical part of any successful real estate investment strategy. By understanding the different types of investment objectives—cash flow, appreciation, tax benefits, and equity building—you can tailor your goals to your financial situation and risk tolerance. Remember, setting SMART goals will help you stay focused and motivated, and regularly reviewing your progress will keep you on track. With a clear roadmap in hand, you're better equipped to navigate the world of real estate investing and build lasting wealth over time.

Financing Your First Deal

Financing your first real estate deal is one of the most critical aspects of getting started in the investment world. The right financing strategy can set the stage for long-term success, while the wrong approach can lead to financial strain and missed opportunities. In this chapter, we will explore the various financing options available to first-time investors, including conventional loans, hard money lenders, and private financing. You'll learn the advantages and disadvantages of each method, helping you make the best choice based on your unique financial situation and investment goals.

1. Conventional Loans

Conventional loans are the most common form of financing for first-time real estate investors. These loans are provided by banks or other traditional lenders and typically require a good credit score, a stable income, and a down payment of at least 20% for investment properties.

a. Benefits of Conventional Loans:

Low Interest Rates: Conventional loans usually offer the lowest interest rates compared to other types of financing, especially if you have a strong credit history and financial background.

Longer Terms: These loans typically come with 15- to 30-year terms, allowing you to spread the cost of your property over a longer period, which can make monthly payments more manageable.

Predictable Payments: Fixed-rate loans offer predictable monthly payments, helping you better plan your cash flow.

Accessibility: With proper documentation, conventional loans are relatively easy to access, especially for those with good credit and financial standing.

b. Challenges of Conventional Loans:

Strict Qualification Requirements: Lenders often have strict requirements for approval, including high credit scores (usually above 650), a debt-to-income ratio (DTI) below 40-45%, and solid income verification.

Down Payment: A 20% down payment is standard for investment properties, which can be a substantial barrier for first-time investors.

Long Processing Time: The application process for conventional loans can take several weeks to months, which can delay your ability to close a deal quickly, especially in a competitive market.

c. When to Use Conventional Loans:

If you have good credit, steady income, and enough savings for a down payment, conventional loans can be an excellent way to finance your first investment property. They offer the lowest interest rates and long-term stability, making them a solid option for investors planning to hold properties for the long run.

2. Hard Money Loans

Hard money loans are short-term, high-interest loans typically offered by private lenders or investors rather than traditional banks. These loans are secured by the property itself, meaning if you default on the loan, the lender can seize the property. Hard money loans are commonly used by investors looking for quick financing for fix-and-flip projects.

a. Benefits of Hard Money Loans:

Fast Approval and Funding: One of the biggest advantages of hard money loans is the speed at which you can secure financing. The process can take as little as a few days, which is ideal for investors who need quick access to capital.

Flexible Terms: Hard money lenders often have more flexible terms than traditional banks, as they focus more on the value of the property rather than your creditworthiness.

Less Stringent Qualification: Hard money lenders are primarily concerned with the collateral (the property) rather than your credit score, so they may be more willing to lend to those with less-than-perfect credit or new investors.

b. Challenges of Hard Money Loans:

Higher Interest Rates: Interest rates for hard money loans can be significantly higher than conventional loans, often ranging from 8% to 15%, depending on the lender and your risk profile.

Shorter Loan Terms: These loans typically come with shorter repayment terms, ranging from six months to a few years. While this is fine for a fix-and-flip investment, it can be a challenge for buy-and-hold investors who need longer repayment periods.

Risk of Losing Property: Since hard money loans are secured by the property, failure to repay the loan could result in losing the investment.

c. When to Use Hard Money Loans:

Hard money loans are ideal for real estate investors who need fast access to capital, especially for short-term projects like flipping properties or buying distressed properties. These loans can also be useful for investors who may not qualify for conventional loans due to a lack of credit history or other factors.

3. Private Financing

Private financing involves borrowing money from private individuals, such as friends, family, or private investors. Unlike institutional lenders, private lenders often have more flexible terms and may be more willing to take a chance on a new investor. The terms of the loan are typically negotiated directly between the borrower and the lender.

a. Benefits of Private Financing:

Flexible Terms: Private lenders are often more flexible with loan terms, interest rates, and repayment schedules. This flexibility can be especially beneficial for first-time investors who may not meet the strict criteria of traditional lenders.

Faster Approval Process: Similar to hard money loans, private loans can be processed quickly, sometimes even within a few days.

Creative Financing Options: Private financing opens the door for creative options, such as seller financing, joint ventures, or partnership arrangements that can help reduce the financial burden on you.

b. Challenges of Private Financing:

High Interest Rates: While private loans can offer flexibility, the interest rates may be higher than conventional loans. Rates can vary widely depending on the lender and the relationship between the borrower and lender.

Potential Strain on Relationships: Borrowing from friends or family can be risky, as it can create personal tension if the investment does not work out. It's essential to establish clear terms in writing to avoid misunderstandings and protect relationships.

Limited Availability: Private financing is not always easy to secure, as it relies on your network and connections. It may take time to find a reliable private lender willing to invest in your deal.

c. When to Use Private Financing:

Private financing is ideal if you have access to a reliable network of individuals willing to lend you money or partner with you on investments. This can be a great option if you need more flexibility than traditional banks offer and are comfortable negotiating the terms directly with the lender.

4. Other Financing Options

While conventional loans, hard money loans, and private financing are the most common methods, there are other ways to finance real estate investments. These include:

a. FHA Loans

First-time buyers can use Federal Housing Administration

(FHA) loans, which are government-backed loans with low down payment requirements (as low as 3.5%). While these loans are typically used for owner-occupied properties, they can also be used for multi-family properties if you live in one unit.

b. Seller Financing

In seller financing, the property seller acts as the lender, and you make payments directly to them instead of a bank. This can be a good option for buyers who may not qualify for traditional financing.

c. Home Equity Lines of Credit (HELOC)

If you already own property, you may be able to use a HELOC to tap into the equity in your current home to fund your investment. This option allows you to borrow against the equity you've built up, often at lower interest rates.

5. Choosing the Right Financing Option

Choosing the right financing option depends on several factors, including your credit history, available capital, the type of property you're buying, and your long-term investment strategy.

If you plan to buy and hold a property for the long term, conventional loans may offer the best rates and terms.

If you're focused on short-term projects like flipping houses, hard money loans could be a better fit due to their speed and flexibility.

If you're new to investing and have limited access to traditional funding, private financing from friends, family, or private investors may be the way to go.

Financing your first real estate deal is a crucial step in your investment journey. Understanding the various financing options available—conventional loans, hard money loans, and private financing—will help you make an informed decision that aligns with your financial goals and risk tolerance. Each option has its own benefits and challenges, so take the time to evaluate your situation and choose the one that best suits your needs. By selecting the right financing strategy, you'll be better positioned to successfully navigate your first deal and set the foundation for future real estate investments.

The Importance of Credit in Real Estate Investing

In the world of real estate investing, your credit score is one of the most important factors that lenders consider when deciding whether to approve your loan application. It not only affects the types of financing options available to you but also the terms and interest rates that will apply. Understanding the role of your credit score in securing financing, as well as how to improve it, is crucial for anyone looking to succeed in real estate investing. In this chapter, we'll explore the impact of credit on real estate investment opportunities, and provide strategies to improve your score before you pursue your first deal.

1. How Credit Affects Real Estate Financing

Lenders use your credit score to assess your creditworthiness, which is an indicator of how likely you are to repay borrowed money. The higher your score, the more likely you are to qualify for favorable loan terms, such as lower interest rates and higher borrowing limits. A good credit score can make the difference between getting approved for a loan and being denied, and between securing affordable financing or being burdened with high-interest rates.

a. Types of Loans and Credit Score Requirements:

Conventional Loans: These loans typically require a credit score of at least 620-650. The higher your score, the more competitive your interest rate will be. Scores above 740 are ideal for securing the best rates.

FHA Loans: These government-backed loans may be available to individuals with a credit score as low as 580, making them a viable option for first-time homebuyers or those with less-than-perfect credit. However, scores under 620 may require a larger down payment.

Hard Money Loans: These loans are less dependent on credit scores since they're secured by the property itself. However, a higher credit score may still help you secure better terms, such as a lower interest rate.

Private Financing: The credit requirements for private loans can vary greatly, depending on the lender. While some private lenders may be more lenient with credit, having a strong score will still increase your chances of getting approved and securing favorable terms.

b. Impact on Interest Rates and Terms:

A good credit score can help you secure financing at lower

interest rates, which will reduce your monthly payments and make your investment more profitable over time. On the other hand, a poor credit score could lead to higher interest rates, making it more expensive to finance your investment and potentially limiting the number of lenders willing to work with you.

2. Why Credit Matters in Real Estate Investing

Credit is crucial in real estate investing because it can directly influence your ability to get funding for your deals, and the cost of that funding. Here are several ways in which your credit score can impact your real estate investment journey:

a. Access to Capital:

In many cases, especially for first-time investors, securing financing for a property will be difficult without a good credit score. Many lenders, including banks and mortgage companies, rely on your credit report to evaluate your financial behavior and determine whether you're a reliable borrower. If your score is low, lenders may be hesitant to lend to you, or they may impose stricter conditions, such as requiring a higher down payment.

b. Loan Terms:

Even if you qualify for a loan with a lower credit score, the terms are likely to be less favorable. For instance, you may be offered a loan with a higher interest rate, which will result in higher monthly payments and a more expensive long-term investment. In contrast, a good credit score can help you secure lower rates and longer repayment terms, improving your cash flow and increasing your return on investment (ROI).

c. Lender Confidence:

Lenders want to feel confident that they will get their money back, and a strong credit score signals to them that you are a responsible borrower. This confidence can lead to quicker approval times and smoother transactions. Conversely, a poor credit history may raise red flags, potentially causing delays or denials of your loan application.

3. Strategies for Improving Your Credit Score

Improving your credit score before applying for a real estate loan can significantly impact your ability to secure financing at favorable rates. While it may take time to see substantial improvements, there are several strategies you can implement to boost your score and increase your chances of getting approved for a loan.

a. Pay Your Bills on Time:

Your payment history accounts for the largest portion of your credit score. Late payments or missed bills can have a significant negative impact. Consistently paying your bills on time is one of the most effective ways to raise your credit score. Set up automatic payments or reminders to ensure that payments are made on time.

b. Reduce Your Credit Utilization:

Credit utilization refers to the percentage of your available credit that you are currently using. A high credit utilization ratio (over 30%) can negatively affect your score. Pay down credit card balances or work to keep your credit utilization below 30% to improve your score.

c. Check Your Credit Report for Errors:

Mistakes on your credit report can unfairly lower your score. Regularly review your credit report for any inaccuracies, such as incorrect late payments, accounts that don't belong to you, or data that hasn't been updated. If you find errors, dispute them with the credit bureaus to have them corrected.

d. Diversify Your Credit Mix:

A healthy mix of credit types—such as credit cards, installment loans, and mortgages—can improve your score. Avoid opening too many new accounts in a short period, as this can negatively affect your score. Instead, focus on maintaining existing accounts and making timely payments.

e. Negotiate with Creditors:

If you have existing debt that is hurting your credit score, consider negotiating with your creditors for more favorable repayment terms, such as lower interest rates or extended payment periods. In some cases, creditors may be willing to remove negative marks from your credit report in exchange for a payment settlement.

4. The Role of Credit in Investment Strategies

Your credit score doesn't just influence the types of loans available to you—it can also affect the kinds of investment strategies you pursue. A higher credit score can open doors to more financing options, enabling you to explore a wider range of investment opportunities.

a. Leveraging Other People's Money (OPM):

If your credit is strong, you may be able to leverage other people's money to finance deals. For instance, lenders may be more willing to offer you favorable terms if they know you have a track record of managing debt responsibly. This can allow you to invest in more properties, diversify your portfolio, and scale your real estate business more quickly.

b. Cash Flow Considerations:

A better credit score means lower interest rates, which leads to better cash flow. With lower monthly payments, you'll have more financial flexibility to reinvest profits into additional properties, renovations, or other investments. This can ultimately lead to a faster accumulation of wealth and more successful investments.

5. When to Apply for a Loan

Knowing when to apply for a loan is just as important as the loan itself. If your credit is still a work in progress, it may be worth waiting to apply for financing until your score is higher. Rushing to secure financing with a poor credit score could result in higher interest rates or a loan denial, which could delay your investment goals.

Your credit score plays a pivotal role in the success of your real estate investing journey. A higher credit score opens up more favorable financing options, allowing you to secure better terms and more favorable interest rates. By understanding how credit works and taking steps to improve your score, you can increase your chances of getting approved for loans, reduce your borrowing costs, and set yourself up for long-term success in the real estate market.

Understanding Leverage in Real Estate

Leverage is one of the most powerful tools in real estate investing. It allows you to amplify your returns by using borrowed money to finance the purchase of a property. In simple terms, leverage involves using other people's money—whether it's from banks, private lenders, or financial institutions—to increase the potential profitability of an investment. However, while leverage can be incredibly beneficial, it also carries risks. In this chapter, we'll break down how leverage works, its benefits and risks, and how to use it wisely to maximize returns while minimizing potential downsides.

1. What is Leverage in Real Estate?

Leverage in real estate refers to the practice of using borrowed funds to finance the purchase of a property, rather than using all of your own capital. Essentially, leverage allows you to control a larger asset with a smaller upfront investment. This means that instead of using 100% of your own money to buy a property, you may only need to contribute a fraction of the total cost, with the rest being covered by a loan.

For example, let's say you're purchasing a property worth $200,000. If you only need to put down $40,000 as a down payment and borrow the remaining $160,000, you're leveraging $160,000 of borrowed money to control the full value of the property. This gives you the opportunity to earn returns on the entire $200,000 value, not just your $40,000 investment.

2. How Leverage Works in Real Estate Investing

Leverage works by amplifying both potential gains and potential losses. If the property value increases, you earn a return on the entire value of the property, not just your initial down payment. However, if the property value decreases, you are still on the hook for repaying the borrowed money.

a. Appreciation:

When property values increase, the gains are multiplied by the amount of leverage you use. For instance, if the property value increases by 10%, and you used 80% leverage, your return on investment (ROI) will be far greater than if you had used all of your own money.

Example:

Property purchase price: $200,000

Loan amount: $160,000 (80% leverage)

Down payment: $40,000 (20% of the total cost)

Property appreciation: 10% ($20,000 increase in value)

Without leverage, your 10% appreciation would result in a $20,000 gain. But with leverage, you gain $20,000 on a $200,000 property with only a $40,000 initial investment, which represents a 50% return on your down payment.

b. Rental Income:

Another way leverage works is through rental income. The money you borrow allows you to acquire a property that generates cash flow through rent. The rental income can be used to cover the property's mortgage payments, operating costs, and potentially provide positive cash flow.

If your rental income exceeds the cost of the mortgage and expenses, you'll make a profit, and again, the return on your investment is amplified by the leverage. However, if rental income does not cover expenses or mortgage payments, you could find yourself in a negative cash flow situation.

3. The Benefits of Leverage in Real Estate

Leverage, when used correctly, offers several key advantages for real estate investors.

a. Increased Return on Investment (ROI):

Leverage is one of the most effective ways to increase your ROI. By using borrowed funds, you can earn a return on a much larger investment than you could with your own capital alone. This enables you to grow your portfolio faster and generate higher profits in a shorter time frame.

b. Tax Benefits:

In many countries, including the United States, mortgage interest on investment properties is tax-deductible. This can reduce the overall cost of borrowing and improve your after-tax returns. Additionally, other property-related expenses, such as repairs and property management fees, may also be deductible.

c. Diversification:

Leverage allows you to diversify your investment portfolio by giving you access to more properties without having to tie up all of your capital. Instead of purchasing a single property with your own funds, you can use leverage to acquire multiple properties, thereby reducing your risk through diversification.

d. Cash Flow:

Leverage allows you to purchase rental properties that generate monthly cash flow. As long as the rental income exceeds your expenses, including the mortgage, maintenance, taxes, and insurance, you can enjoy a steady stream of passive income. This makes real estate a more attractive investment for those seeking regular cash flow.

4. The Risks of Leverage in Real Estate

While leverage can increase your returns, it also amplifies risk. Using borrowed money means you're taking on debt, which must be repaid regardless of the performance of your investment. If your property's value decreases, or if rental income fails to cover your expenses, you could face financial difficulties.

a. Market Downturns:

Real estate markets are cyclical, and they can experience downturns. If the value of your property decreases and you are heavily leveraged, you could owe more on your mortgage than the property is worth (negative equity). In such cases, it can be difficult to sell the property without incurring a loss.

b. Negative Cash Flow:

If your rental income doesn't cover the mortgage and operating expenses, you could be left with negative cash flow. This means you'd need to cover the shortfall out of pocket, which can drain your finances over time. If you are relying too heavily on leverage, this situation can quickly become financially unsustainable.

c. Interest Rate Risk:

Leverage often involves taking on debt with a fixed or variable interest rate. If interest rates rise, your monthly mortgage payments could increase, leading to higher costs and potentially eroding your profits. For investors with variable-rate loans, rising interest rates can significantly impact cash flow and profitability.

d. Debt Obligation:

Regardless of how well or poorly the property performs, you're still obligated to repay the borrowed money. Missing payments or defaulting on your loan can lead to foreclosure, and damage your credit, which could impact your ability to secure future loans.

5. How to Use Leverage Wisely

To maximize the benefits of leverage while minimizing the risks, it's essential to use it wisely. Here are some strategies to ensure that leverage works in your favor:

a. Start Small and Gradually Scale Up:

If you're new to real estate investing, it's often best to start with a smaller, manageable investment and use moderate leverage. As you gain experience and build equity, you can increase your leverage and purchase more properties.

b. Evaluate Property Cash Flow:

Before leveraging a property, ensure that the rental income is sufficient to cover all expenses, including the mortgage, property taxes, maintenance, and insurance. Having a positive cash flow will ensure that you can make your payments even if your property's value decreases.

c. Maintain a Healthy Debt-to-Income Ratio:

A healthy debt-to-income (DTI) ratio is essential when using leverage. Lenders typically look for a DTI of 36% or lower when approving loans. Keeping your DTI ratio under control helps you avoid overleveraging, which could strain your finances.

d. Have a Contingency Plan:

Always have a contingency plan in place in case the market turns or your rental income doesn't cover expenses. Having an emergency fund or an alternative source of income can help you weather tough times without risking your investment.

Leverage is a powerful tool in real estate investing, offering the potential to increase returns, diversify your portfolio, and generate cash flow. However, it's important to understand both the advantages and the risks involved in using leverage. By using borrowed capital wisely, maintaining a conservative approach, and thoroughly evaluating each investment, you can effectively use leverage to amplify your success in the real estate market while minimizing the potential downsides.

Conducting Market Research

Successful real estate investing begins with thorough market research. Understanding the dynamics of a real estate market enables you to identify profitable investment opportunities and minimize risks. By analyzing market trends, job growth, population changes, and other critical factors, you can pinpoint locations that offer the best potential for returns. In this chapter, we'll explore the key steps and tools for conducting effective market research to ensure your investments are well-informed and strategically placed.

1. Why Market Research Matters

Market research helps you determine where to invest and what type of property to invest in. A well-researched market can provide higher appreciation, consistent rental demand, and reduced risk of vacancy. Conversely, neglecting this step can result in poor investment choices, leading to financial losses. By understanding the factors that drive real estate markets, you position yourself to make smarter, more profitable decisions.

2. Key Factors to Analyze

a. Economic Indicators

Economic growth is a major driver of real estate markets. Look for areas with rising employment rates, diverse industries, and strong job creation. A growing economy typically translates to increased demand for housing and commercial spaces.

b. Population Trends

Demographics play a crucial role in real estate. Areas with increasing populations often experience higher housing demand. Pay attention to factors such as population growth, age distribution, and migration patterns, as these can indicate long-term investment potential.

c. Supply and Demand

A balanced market ensures property values remain stable or grow. Research the inventory of available properties in the area and compare it to the demand. Markets with high demand and limited supply often provide better appreciation and rental income opportunities.

d. Infrastructure Development

Upcoming infrastructure projects, such as new highways, public transportation, or commercial centers, can significantly boost property values in an area. Keep an eye on government or private development plans that could make a location more desirable in the future.

e. Neighborhood Quality

Not all neighborhoods within a market offer the same potential. Investigate school ratings, crime rates, amenities, and overall quality of life in specific areas. Properties in neighborhoods with good schools and low crime rates tend to attract higher demand.

3. Research Tools and Resources

a. Online Marketplaces and Platforms

Websites like Zillow, Realtor.com, and Redfin provide valuable insights into property values, rental trends, and market conditions. These platforms can help you analyze listings and pricing trends.

b. Government Data

Access government resources such as census data, labor statistics, and economic reports to gain insights into population growth, employment rates, and income levels in your target market.

c. Local Real Estate Agents and Professionals

Engage with local real estate agents, appraisers, or property managers who have in-depth knowledge of the area. Their expertise can offer insights beyond raw data, including market nuances and hidden opportunities.

d. Walk the Area

Nothing beats firsthand observation. Visit the location, interact with residents, and observe the condition of properties and infrastructure. A physical presence helps you assess the area's desirability more effectively.

e. Comparative Market Analysis (CMA)

A CMA compares recently sold properties in the area to estimate a property's fair market value. This tool is particularly useful for understanding pricing trends and determining the potential return on investment.

4. Identifying Emerging Markets

Emerging markets offer some of the best opportunities for real estate investors. These are locations on the verge of rapid growth due to factors like increased job opportunities, infrastructure development, or affordability compared to neighboring cities. Identifying such markets early can result in significant returns as demand outpaces supply.

Key signs of an emerging market include:

Increasing rent and property prices

Announcements of large-scale projects (e.g., tech hubs or corporate offices)

Migration from other high-cost areas

5. Red Flags to Watch For

While researching markets, be mindful of warning signs that could indicate potential problems. Declining populations, high unemployment rates, and over-saturated markets often pose greater risks. Additionally, be cautious in areas heavily reliant on a single industry, as economic downturns in that sector can severely impact property values.

6. Creating a Market Research Strategy

a. Define Your Investment Goals

Your research should align with your goals. For example, if you're looking for cash flow, prioritize markets with high rental demand. For appreciation, focus on areas poised for growth.

b. Analyze Multiple Markets

Don't limit yourself to your immediate location. Expanding your search to neighboring cities or even states can uncover better opportunities.

c. Combine Data with Intuition

While data is critical, don't discount your instincts. An area that "feels right" based on your observations and research might just be the next hot spot.

Market research is the foundation of successful real estate investing. By understanding economic indicators, population trends, supply and demand, and infrastructure development, you can identify profitable opportunities and avoid costly mistakes. Armed with the right tools and strategies, you'll be able to make data-driven decisions that align with your investment goals. With solid research, you're not just investing in property—you're investing in your financial future.

Analyzing Potential Properties

Evaluating a property before purchase is a crucial step in real estate investing. A thorough analysis helps determine whether a property aligns with your investment goals and has the potential to yield desirable returns. In this chapter, we'll outline the key factors to consider when analyzing a property, ensuring you make well-informed decisions.

1. Understanding the Importance of Property Analysis

Analyzing potential properties minimizes risks and ensures you don't overpay. It allows you to assess the property's potential for cash flow, appreciation, and overall profitability. A detailed evaluation also uncovers any red flags that may impact future returns.

2. Key Factors to Consider

a. Location

Location remains the most critical factor in real estate. A

property in a desirable area with proximity to schools, transportation, amenities, and employment hubs often commands higher demand and retains value. Research neighborhood trends, such as gentrification or declining conditions, to gauge long-term potential.

b. Property Condition

Inspect the property for structural integrity, plumbing, electrical systems, roofing, and overall maintenance. Properties in poor condition may require costly repairs, eating into your profits. Use professional inspections to identify hidden issues.

c. Rental Income Potential

For buy-and-hold investors, rental income is a primary consideration. Analyze local rental market trends to estimate monthly income. Compare this figure to the property's costs (mortgage, taxes, insurance, and maintenance) to determine cash flow potential.

d. Comparable Market Analysis (CMA)

Study comparable properties (or "comps") recently sold or rented in the area. Comps provide insight into the property's fair market value and rental potential. Look for properties with similar size, age, and location for the most accurate comparisons.

e. Investment Metrics

Cap Rate: Measures the annual return based on the property's net operating income (NOI) divided by its purchase price. Higher cap rates typically indicate better investment potential.

Cash-on-Cash Return: Evaluates the return on your invested cash, ideal for understanding short-term gains.

Gross Rent Multiplier (GRM): The ratio of the property's price to its annual rental income, useful for quick evaluations.

f. Future Development Plans

Investigate upcoming developments in the area, such as new infrastructure, businesses, or zoning changes. These projects can enhance property values and rental demand, making the investment more lucrative.

g. Market Trends

Study the local market's current phase within the real estate cycle (expansion, peak, contraction, recovery). Knowing the market's trajectory can help you time your investment effectively.

3. Steps for Conducting a Property Analysis

a. Start with Online Research

Utilize platforms like Zillow or Realtor.com to gather data on the property, including price history, neighborhood insights, and comparable listings.

b. Visit the Property

A physical visit allows you to assess the property's condition, location, and overall appeal. Take note of potential repairs and how the property compares to others in the area.

c. Hire a Professional Inspector

A property inspector can identify structural issues, code violations, or hidden problems that might not be immediately visible.

d. Evaluate Financials

Calculate all costs associated with the property, including purchase price, closing costs, renovation expenses, and ongoing expenses like property management fees and maintenance. Compare these against projected income.

e. Consult Experts

Engage with real estate agents, property managers, and local market experts to gather additional insights about the property's potential.

4. Red Flags to Avoid

a. Overpriced Properties

Properties priced significantly higher than comps may be difficult to resell or rent profitably. Avoid properties where the numbers don't add up.

b. High Vacancy Rates in the Area

A high vacancy rate suggests a weak rental market, which could make finding tenants challenging.

c. Major Repairs Needed

Properties requiring extensive renovations can quickly exceed your budget and timeline, especially for inexperienced investors.

d. One-Industry Towns

Avoid areas heavily reliant on a single industry, as economic downturns in that sector could severely impact property demand.

5. Using Technology in Property Analysis

Modern tools make property analysis more accessible. Platforms like PropStream and Mashvisor offer detailed analytics, helping investors evaluate properties' financial viability. These tools provide data on rental income, expenses, ROI projections, and more, saving time and enhancing accuracy.

6. The Final Decision

After completing your analysis, compare the property's potential returns to your investment goals. If the numbers align and the property shows promise for appreciation, cash flow, or both, it may be a strong candidate. Remember, patience is key—don't rush into deals that don't meet your criteria.

Analyzing potential properties is a skill that improves with experience. By carefully considering location, condition, rental potential, and financial metrics, you can make informed decisions that maximize your returns and minimize risks. With each analysis, you'll gain confidence and refine your ability to identify the best investment opportunities.

Rental Property Investing

Investing in rental properties is a popular strategy for generating steady income and building long-term wealth. However, it requires careful planning and hands-on management to succeed. In this chapter, we'll delve into the essentials of rental property investing, exploring its advantages, challenges, and best practices for effective management.

1. Why Choose Rental Properties?

Rental properties offer multiple benefits:

Cash Flow: Monthly rental income provides a steady revenue stream, often exceeding property expenses.

Appreciation: Over time, property values typically increase, adding to your overall wealth.

Tax Advantages: Expenses like mortgage interest, property management fees, and repairs can be deducted from your taxable income.

Portfolio Diversification: Rental properties add a tangible asset class to your investment portfolio.

2. Types of Rental Properties

a. Single-Family Homes

Ideal for beginners, these properties are simpler to manage and attract long-term tenants.

b. Multi-Family Units

Duplexes, triplexes, and apartment buildings generate multiple income streams but require more management effort.

c. Short-Term Rentals

Platforms like Airbnb make short-term rentals appealing, though they demand frequent tenant turnover and higher upkeep.

3. Key Considerations Before Investing

a. Understanding Local Markets

Research neighborhoods with strong rental demand, low vacancy rates, and access to schools, transport, and amenities.

b. Analyzing Financials

Use metrics like cash-on-cash return, cap rate, and GRM to assess a property's profitability. Ensure monthly income exceeds expenses for positive cash flow.

c. Legal and Regulatory Knowledge

Understand local landlord-tenant laws, zoning regulations, and short-term rental restrictions before investing.

4. Tenant Management

a. Tenant Screening

Thorough screening minimizes issues. Verify income, credit history, and references to ensure tenants can pay rent and maintain the property.

b. Lease Agreements

Craft a comprehensive lease covering rent amounts, payment schedules, security deposits, and tenant responsibilities.

c. Maintaining Good Relationships

Clear communication fosters trust. Respond promptly to tenant concerns to encourage long-term occupancy.

5. Property Maintenance

a. Routine Upkeep

Schedule regular inspections to identify and address issues early. Maintenance includes plumbing, electrical systems, and HVAC servicing.

b. Emergency Repairs

Plan for unexpected repairs. A reserve fund ensures you can address emergencies without financial strain.

c. Outsourcing vs. DIY

Decide whether to manage the property yourself or hire a property management company. While self-management saves money, professional managers can reduce stress and handle tenant interactions efficiently.

6. Challenges in Rental Property Investing

a. Vacancy Periods

Unoccupied properties generate no income but still incur costs. Mitigate this by marketing the property aggressively and pricing competitively.

b. Problematic Tenants

Non-payment or property damage can disrupt cash flow. Effective screening and legal recourse are essential.

c. Maintenance Costs

Repairs can be unpredictable and expensive. Budgeting for ongoing maintenance is crucial.

7. Scaling Your Rental Property Portfolio

a. Refinancing and Leverage

Use equity from one property to finance additional purchases. Leverage allows you to grow your portfolio without significant out-of-pocket expenses.

b. Diversification

Invest in different property types or locations to spread risk and maximize returns.

c. Building a Team

As you scale, assemble a reliable team, including real estate agents, contractors, and accountants, to streamline operations.

Rental property investing can be a rewarding venture with proper planning and management. By understanding market dynamics, maintaining your property, and building strong tenant relationships, you can enjoy consistent income and long-term growth. Success in rental property investing lies in balancing risks with opportunities and continuously learning from your experiences.

Flipping Houses for Profit

Flipping houses is a high-reward real estate investment strategy that involves buying distressed properties, renovating them, and selling them for a profit. This strategy has attracted many investors due to the potential for quick gains, but it also requires significant knowledge, skills, and capital to be successful. In this chapter, we'll walk through the entire house-flipping process, from property selection to renovations and selling.

1. Why Flip Houses?

Flipping houses can be a lucrative endeavor, offering several benefits:

Fast Profits: Unlike rental properties, which provide long-term gains, flipping houses can generate substantial profits in a short period, often within a few months.

Building Wealth: By consistently flipping houses, you can build substantial wealth over time if you make smart investments and manage your costs effectively.

Control Over Property Value: Unlike other investment strategies, flipping houses allows you to actively influence the value of the property through renovations.

2. Selecting the Right Property to Flip

The first and most critical step in flipping houses is choosing the right property. A successful flip begins with a well-chosen investment. Here's what to look for:

a. Location

Location is one of the most important factors when selecting a property to flip. Look for homes in neighborhoods with growing demand and potential for appreciation. Proximity to schools, shopping, transportation, and other amenities increases property value.

b. Market Research

Analyze local market trends. Look for areas with increasing home prices, low crime rates, and demand for renovated homes. Make sure there's a demand for homes within the price range after renovations.

c. Distressed Properties

Flipping works best with properties that are undervalued due to condition or cosmetic issues. Look for properties in need of repairs or updates, such as older homes with outdated features or properties in foreclosure. Avoid homes that require extensive structural repairs unless you have experience in those areas.

d. Buy Below Market Value

To ensure profitability, you must purchase properties at below market value. This allows room for renovation costs and profit once the property is sold. A good rule of thumb is the 70% rule: purchase the property for no more than 70% of its after-repair value (ARV), minus renovation costs.

3. Planning Renovations

Once you've purchased the property, the next step is planning your renovations. The goal is to increase the home's value while staying within your budget and timeline.

a. Budgeting for Renovations

A well-detailed budget is crucial to a successful flip. Make sure to factor in all costs, including labor, materials, permits, and unexpected issues. It's wise to leave some room for contingencies, as renovation projects often go over budget.

b. High-Return Renovations

Focus on renovations that yield the highest return on investment (ROI). These typically include:

Kitchen and Bathroom Upgrades: These are the most important rooms in a home and often lead to significant value increases.

Curb Appeal: First impressions matter. Improving the exterior with landscaping, a fresh coat of paint, and a new front door can drastically increase the property's value.

Flooring and Paint: A fresh coat of paint and new flooring can completely transform a property without breaking the bank.

c. Avoid Over-Improving

While it's tempting to go all out with luxury features, over-improving can lead to diminishing returns. Focus on quality, functional renovations that align with the area's average home prices. For example, adding a pool or high-end appliances may not provide the same ROI in a middle-class neighborhood as it would in a luxury area.

d. Hiring Contractors

If you're not experienced in renovations, hiring reliable contractors is essential. Ensure they are licensed, insured, and have a proven track record. Work closely with your contractors to ensure the project stays on schedule and within budget.

4. Selling the Property

Once renovations are complete, it's time to sell the property. The goal is to sell quickly at a profit, so timing and presentation are key.

a. Pricing the Property

To set the right price, compare your home to similar recently sold properties (comps) in the area. Consider factors such as location, size, and amenities when setting your listing price. Pricing too high can lead to long market exposure, while pricing too low may leave money on the table.

b. Staging and Marketing

Staging the property can make a significant difference in how quickly it sells. Professional staging can highlight the home's best features and make it more appealing to potential buyers. Ensure the property is clean, well-maintained, and free of clutter.

Marketing is also crucial. Use high-quality photos, virtual tours, and targeted online ads to attract potential buyers. Work with a skilled real estate agent who understands the local market to help you list and negotiate.

c. Negotiating and Closing

Be prepared to negotiate with buyers. Buyers may request repairs or adjustments before finalizing the sale. It's important to know your bottom line and be prepared to walk away if the deal isn't right.

Once an agreement is reached, the closing process begins.

This includes signing contracts, completing inspections, and transferring ownership. Work with a real estate attorney or agent to ensure the closing goes smoothly.

5. Challenges in Flipping Houses

Flipping houses comes with several challenges that investors need to be aware of:

Unforeseen Costs: Renovation costs can exceed expectations, especially if the property has hidden issues like mold or foundation problems.

Market Conditions: Market fluctuations can affect the selling price. It's crucial to have a clear understanding of current market conditions.

Time Constraints: Flipping houses requires a quick turnaround. Delays in renovations or sales can eat into your profits.

6. Strategies for Success in Flipping Houses

To maximize your chances of success, consider these strategies:

Work with a Real Estate Agent: A knowledgeable agent can help you find properties at a good price, assist with market analysis, and negotiate the sale.

Start Small: If you're new to flipping, start with a small

property or a less complicated renovation project. Gain experience before moving on to larger, more complex flips.

Build a Team: Having a reliable team of contractors, inspectors, and real estate agents will help streamline the flipping process and ensure everything runs smoothly.

Flipping houses for profit can be a rewarding strategy when approached with knowledge and preparation. By carefully selecting properties, budgeting effectively for renovations, and marketing the finished product, you can turn a distressed home into a profitable asset. However, successful house flipping requires diligence, market awareness, and the ability to handle risks. If done right, flipping houses can provide quick returns and help you grow your real estate portfolio.

Understanding Real Estate Taxes

Real estate taxes are an essential part of real estate investing that can significantly impact your overall returns. While taxes can be a complex topic, understanding the various types of taxes that apply to real estate properties, how they work, and strategies to minimize your tax burden is vital for any investor. In this chapter, we will break down the key tax implications of real estate investing and provide practical strategies for reducing taxes.

1. Types of Real Estate Taxes

Real estate investors need to be familiar with several types of taxes that can apply to properties. These include property taxes, income taxes, capital gains taxes, and others. Each type of tax plays a role in how much an investor will owe after a transaction, and understanding these taxes helps in making better investment decisions.

a. Property Taxes

Property taxes are levied by local governments on real estate properties, typically based on the assessed value of the property. These taxes fund local services, such as schools, emergency services, and infrastructure. Property taxes are usually paid annually or semi-annually and are one of the most consistent expenses for property owners.

Assessment Process: Property taxes are determined by local tax assessors, who assign a value to the property. This assessed value is then multiplied by the local tax rate to calculate the tax liability.

Tax Deductions: In some areas, certain property types, such as primary residences or historic properties, may qualify for tax exemptions or reductions. It's essential to know if any exemptions apply to your properties.

b. Income Taxes on Rental Income

If you invest in rental properties, the income generated from rents is subject to income tax. Rental income must be reported on your tax return, and it is taxed at your ordinary income tax rate.

Deductions: Fortunately, as a real estate investor, you can deduct many expenses associated with maintaining and operating rental properties. This includes mortgage interest, property management fees, repairs, insurance premiums, and utilities. These deductions can significantly reduce your taxable rental income.

Depreciation: One of the most valuable tax benefits for rental property owners is depreciation. Depreciation allows you to deduct a portion of the property's value each year over its useful life (typically 27.5 years for residential properties). This can offset some of your rental income and reduce your overall tax liability.

c. Capital Gains Taxes

Capital gains taxes are incurred when you sell a property for a profit. The gain is the difference between the sale price and the purchase price, minus any costs associated with the sale (e.g., agent fees, closing costs, and renovations).

Short-Term vs. Long-Term Capital Gains: If you sell a property within a year of purchase, the gain is considered short-term and taxed at ordinary income tax rates. If you hold the property for more than a year before selling, the gain is considered long-term and is subject to lower capital gains tax rates, which range from 0% to 20% depending on your income bracket.

1031 Exchange: One way to defer capital gains taxes is through a 1031 exchange. This IRS provision allows you to sell one investment property and purchase another similar property, deferring the tax liability on the gain until you eventually sell the replacement property.

d. Sales Taxes

In some areas, sales tax may apply to specific types of real estate transactions, such as the sale of property improvements or materials. While this tax is not typically a direct cost to the buyer or investor in the way property taxes are, it's important to be aware of its existence if your investments involve significant renovations.

2. Strategies for Reducing Real Estate Taxes

While taxes are a natural part of real estate investing, there are several strategies that investors can use to minimize their tax liabilities and maximize profits. Below are some effective strategies for reducing taxes on your real estate investments.

a. Take Advantage of Deductions

As mentioned earlier, real estate investors can deduct a variety of expenses associated with their properties. These deductions can help lower your taxable income and reduce the overall amount of taxes owed. Some common deductions include:

Mortgage Interest: You can deduct interest paid on mortgages for investment properties.

Property Management Fees: If you hire a property manager, these fees are deductible.

Repairs and Maintenance: Routine maintenance and repairs, such as plumbing or electrical work, are deductible expenses.

Travel Expenses: If you need to travel for property management or to check on your investments, these travel expenses can be deducted.

b. Maximize Depreciation

Depreciation is one of the most powerful tax-saving tools for real estate investors. By depreciating your property over time, you can offset a portion of your rental income, reducing your tax bill. However, it's important to note that when you sell the property, you may be required to "recapture" some of the depreciation as taxable income. Nevertheless, depreciation remains a valuable tool for long-term wealth building.

c. Utilize a 1031 Exchange

A 1031 exchange is a tax-deferral strategy that allows investors to defer paying capital gains taxes on an investment property when it is sold, as long as the proceeds are reinvested in a similar property. This is a powerful way to build wealth without having to pay taxes on the gains, as long as you follow the IRS guidelines and timelines for the exchange.

d. Consider Real Estate Professional Status

If you are a full-time real estate investor, you may qualify for "real estate professional status" under IRS rules. This status allows you to deduct more of your real estate-related expenses from your taxable income, including losses from rental properties. To qualify, you must spend more than 750 hours per year actively involved in real estate activities, and more than half of your total working hours must be spent in real estate.

e. Tax-Advantaged Accounts

Investing through tax-advantaged accounts, such as a self-directed IRA (Individual Retirement Account) or 401(k), can allow you to grow your real estate investments without being subject to immediate taxes on rental income or capital gains. These accounts defer taxes until you withdraw the funds, or in the case of a Roth IRA, allow for tax-free withdrawals once you reach retirement age.

f. Tax Planning and Professional Help

Real estate investors should also consider working with a tax professional who specializes in real estate. A knowledgeable accountant or tax advisor can help you develop a tax strategy tailored to your specific situation, ensuring you take full advantage of available deductions, credits, and deferral strategies.

3. Common Pitfalls to Avoid

While there are numerous strategies to reduce taxes, it's important to avoid some common pitfalls:

Overestimating Deductions: Ensure that your deductions are legitimate and properly documented. Audits are common, and being overly aggressive with deductions can lead to penalties.

Misunderstanding Depreciation Recapture: Be aware that depreciation recapture taxes may apply when you sell a property. This could impact your long-term tax strategy if not carefully planned.

Failure to Track Expenses: Keep detailed records of all expenses related to your investment properties. Failing to track your expenses properly can result in missed deductions and increased tax liabilities.

Understanding real estate taxes is crucial for any investor looking to maximize returns. By familiarizing yourself with the different types of taxes, leveraging available deductions and tax strategies, and seeking professional advice, you can minimize your tax burden and increase the profitability of your real estate investments. With careful tax planning, you can ensure that your real estate investments work for you both financially and strategically, allowing you to build long-term wealth and achieve your investment goals.

Building a Real Estate Investment Team

Real estate investing can be a lucrative venture, but it requires more than just capital and knowledge of the market. A key factor in ensuring success in real estate is building a solid team of professionals who bring expertise to different aspects of the investment process. These experts can help you avoid costly mistakes, streamline operations, and optimize returns. In this chapter, we'll discuss the importance of building a reliable real estate investment team and the key players you need to assemble to ensure your success.

1. The Importance of a Strong Team

Real estate investing involves complex processes, from finding and analyzing properties to financing, negotiating, and managing. While it's possible to handle some of these tasks yourself, many investors find that assembling a strong team of professionals is essential for maximizing their efforts. These experts can bring valuable insights, save time, and help you navigate the challenges that arise in real estate deals.

Leverage Expertise: Real estate deals often involve nuances that can be difficult for beginners to understand. With a team of experienced professionals, you can leverage their expertise to make informed decisions.

Time Efficiency: By outsourcing specific tasks to experts, you free up time to focus on other aspects of your business, like scaling your portfolio or seeking new investment opportunities.

Risk Reduction: Real estate transactions come with financial risks, legal obligations, and operational challenges. Having the right professionals on your side can help minimize these risks and ensure your investments are sound.

2. Key Members of Your Real Estate Investment Team

A successful real estate investment team typically includes a variety of professionals, each with a specific role to help you achieve your investment goals. Here are the essential team members you need to have:

a. Real Estate Agent or Broker

A skilled real estate agent or broker is one of the most important members of your team. These professionals have extensive knowledge of the local market, access to listings, and experience in negotiation.

Market Knowledge: A good agent will understand local trends, including property values, neighborhoods, and upcoming developments that could affect your investment.

Access to Listings: Agents have access to multiple listing services (MLS), which allow them to find properties that might not be publicly listed yet or might be a good investment opportunity.

Negotiation Skills: Experienced agents can help you negotiate favorable prices, terms, and conditions, ensuring you get the best deal possible.

b. Real Estate Attorney

A real estate attorney is essential for handling the legal aspects of your investment, from drafting contracts to reviewing agreements and ensuring that all transactions comply with the law.

Contract Review: A real estate attorney will ensure that any contracts you sign are in your best interest, including sale agreements, rental contracts, and partnership agreements.

Title Issues: They can help you investigate any title issues, such as disputes or liens on a property, and ensure that the title is clear before completing a deal.

Compliance and Litigation: In case you face legal issues, an attorney can help resolve disputes, represent you in court, and ensure that you comply with zoning laws and regulations.

c. Contractors and Handymen

Whether you're flipping houses or managing rental properties, you'll need reliable contractors and handymen to maintain, renovate, or repair properties. Having a trusted network of skilled tradespeople is crucial to keeping your investments in good condition and increasing their value.

Renovations and Repairs: Contractors are essential for handling large-scale renovations, while handymen can tackle smaller, day-to-day maintenance issues.

Cost-Effective Solutions: A good contractor will help you find cost-effective solutions to improve your properties, enhancing their market value without exceeding your budget.

Timeliness: Contractors who can complete jobs on time and within budget are crucial to ensuring that your properties remain rentable or ready for sale quickly.

d. Property Manager

A property manager takes care of the day-to-day operations of your rental properties, relieving you of the time-consuming tasks involved in managing tenants and maintaining the property.

Tenant Management: Property managers screen tenants, handle lease agreements, and address tenant concerns. They also ensure that rental payments are collected on time.

Property Maintenance: They oversee property upkeep, coordinate repairs, and ensure the property remains in good condition.

Legal Compliance: Property managers help ensure compliance with landlord-tenant laws, including fair housing regulations, security deposits, and eviction processes.

e. Lenders and Financial Advisors

Financial professionals, such as lenders and advisors, play an integral role in helping you secure funding for your investments and structure your deals in a way that minimizes risk and maximizes profit.

Lenders: Whether you're securing a mortgage or a hard money loan, lenders are essential for financing your real estate deals. It's important to establish strong relationships with various lenders to find the best financing options for each investment.

Financial Advisors: A financial advisor with real estate experience can help you structure your investments to optimize tax efficiency, balance risk, and set long-term financial goals.

f. Insurance Agent

An insurance agent ensures that your properties are adequately covered in case of unexpected events such as fires, theft, or natural disasters. Insurance is a critical element of risk management for real estate investors.

Property Insurance: This covers damage to the property itself and its contents. It's crucial to have enough coverage to repair or replace the property if necessary.

Liability Insurance: Liability insurance protects you from lawsuits arising from tenant injuries or accidents on your property.

Specialized Coverage: For commercial or multi-family properties, you may need additional coverage like loss of income insurance or flood insurance.

g. Accountants and Tax Professionals

An accountant or tax professional helps you with financial reporting, tax planning, and ensuring that you're meeting all your financial obligations.

Tax Strategy: Accountants help you structure your investments in a way that reduces tax liability, including maximizing deductions, depreciation, and utilizing tax-deferred strategies like 1031 exchanges.

Bookkeeping and Recordkeeping: Accountants assist with keeping detailed records of your income and expenses, ensuring compliance with tax laws and preparing you for tax season.

Financial Reporting: A professional can help you analyze your investment performance, identify potential issues, and develop strategies for growth.

3. Building a Collaborative Team

Once you identify the key players for your team, it's important to ensure that everyone works well together. Communication and collaboration are crucial for success. Here are some tips for fostering a strong team dynamic:

Regular Communication: Hold regular meetings or check-ins with your team to ensure everyone is on the same page and to discuss ongoing projects.

Clear Expectations: Be clear about your expectations for each team member's role and responsibilities.

Create a Trusting Relationship: Build relationships based on trust and respect, and value each team member's expertise. A well-functioning team is more likely to deliver successful outcomes.

Building a real estate investment team is one of the most critical steps to ensure long-term success. Each professional brings unique knowledge and skills that contribute to the growth and sustainability of your investment portfolio. By carefully selecting and nurturing relationships with key team members, you can streamline operations, mitigate risks, and capitalize on opportunities in the real estate market. Your team is the backbone of your real estate business, so take the time to build a team you can trust and rely on. With the right professionals by your side, you'll be well-positioned to navigate the complexities of real estate investing and achieve your financial goals.

The Power of Networking in Real Estate

In the world of real estate investing, success doesn't solely rely on knowledge or capital—networking plays a pivotal role in uncovering new opportunities, building lasting relationships, and staying ahead in the competitive market. By expanding your network, you open doors to valuable resources, industry insights, and potential partnerships. In this chapter, we will explore the power of networking in real estate, effective strategies to connect with other investors and professionals, and how to leverage these connections for long-term success.

1. Why Networking Matters in Real Estate

Real estate is a people-driven business, and building a strong network is one of the most effective ways to gain access to investment opportunities that might not be publicly available. Networking helps you:

Find Hidden Opportunities: Many of the best real estate deals, whether for rental properties, flips, or commercial investments, are often not listed on the open market. Networking with other investors, real estate agents, and brokers can provide access to off-market deals.

Gain Industry Insights: Real estate markets and trends are constantly shifting. By engaging with others in the industry, you can stay informed about market conditions, emerging trends, and new investment strategies.

Collaborate and Scale: Networking opens the door to partnerships, joint ventures, and co-investment opportunities. Whether you're looking for financing, expertise, or shared risk, building relationships with other investors can help you scale your business more quickly.

2. Effective Networking Strategies

There are many ways to build and nurture a network in the real estate sector. Below are some strategies that can help you connect with the right people and leverage these relationships to your advantage:

a. Attend Real Estate Events and Conferences

Industry events, conferences, and meetups are some of the best places to meet like-minded investors, professionals, and experts. These events offer numerous opportunities for networking and learning.

Real Estate Investment Groups (REIGs): Joining a local REIG allows you to meet other investors, share experiences, and discuss market conditions. Many cities have local investment groups that meet regularly to talk shop and share leads.

Conferences and Trade Shows: National and international conferences can connect you with professionals in different sectors of the real estate industry, such as property managers, lenders, contractors, and developers. These events typically feature seminars, workshops, and panel discussions that can expand your knowledge and help you build new relationships.

Workshops and Seminars: Attending educational workshops or seminars is another great way to meet people who share your interests in real estate. These events often focus on specific aspects of real estate investing, such as tax strategies, property management, or flipping houses.

b. Leverage Social Media and Online Platforms

Social media has become an indispensable tool for networking in today's real estate market. Platforms like LinkedIn, Facebook, Instagram, and Twitter provide opportunities to engage with industry professionals and fellow investors.

LinkedIn: This professional network is essential for building your real estate connections. By following and engaging with key industry figures, sharing relevant content, and participating in discussions, you can expand your network and establish yourself as a knowledgeable investor.

Facebook Groups: There are countless Facebook groups

dedicated to real estate investing. Joining these groups allows you to participate in discussions, share tips, ask questions, and connect with both beginners and experienced investors.

Instagram and YouTube: Social media platforms like Instagram and YouTube are increasingly being used by real estate investors to showcase their projects, share tips, and build credibility. Following influencers and engaging with their content can help you stay informed and connect with others.

Online Forums: Real estate forums, such as BiggerPockets or local investment boards, are platforms where investors discuss market trends, share experiences, and provide advice. These platforms are ideal for networking and asking questions, as they attract both new and seasoned investors.

c. Form Partnerships with Other Investors

As a new investor, partnering with more experienced individuals is one of the quickest ways to gain knowledge and access to larger deals. Partnerships allow you to pool resources, share risks, and leverage each other's expertise.

Joint Ventures: Partnering with someone who has complementary skills, such as a contractor or property manager, can help you handle larger projects or manage properties more efficiently. Joint ventures allow you to split costs and profits, making deals more accessible and less risky.

Mentorship: Building relationships with seasoned investors

can provide invaluable insights. A mentor can help guide you through the investment process, advise you on deal structuring, and share lessons learned from their own experience.

d. Build Relationships with Real Estate Professionals

In addition to networking with other investors, establishing relationships with key real estate professionals can significantly benefit your investment strategy. These include:

Real Estate Agents: Agents who specialize in investment properties have access to exclusive listings and can provide invaluable market insights. By developing strong relationships with agents, you can gain access to properties before they hit the public market.

Lenders and Mortgage Brokers: Real estate financing can be complex, and having reliable connections with lenders or mortgage brokers is crucial. Networking with these professionals can give you access to favorable loan terms and help you secure funding for your deals.

Contractors and Property Managers: Having reliable contractors and property managers on your team can make a huge difference in your investment success. Building relationships with trusted professionals ensures that you can rely on them for quick, quality work when needed.

Insurance Agents: Insurance is an essential aspect of real estate investing. Networking with insurance professionals can help you find affordable, comprehensive coverage for your properties.

3. Networking Tips for Success

Effective networking doesn't just involve attending events or connecting online; it also requires building authentic relationships. Below are a few tips for successful networking:

Be Genuine: Authenticity goes a long way in building trust with others. Instead of focusing on what you can gain from a connection, approach networking as a way to learn, share, and build mutually beneficial relationships.

Follow Up: After meeting someone at an event or connecting online, always follow up. A simple email or message expressing your appreciation for the conversation can help solidify the relationship and set the stage for future interactions.

Provide Value: Networking is a two-way street. Think about how you can offer value to others, whether it's sharing your knowledge, offering introductions, or providing helpful resources. The more value you offer, the more your network will grow.

Stay Consistent: Networking is not a one-time activity; it requires consistency. Make a habit of engaging with your network regularly through social media, emails, or even in-person check-ins.

Networking is one of the most powerful tools at your disposal as a real estate investor. By building and maintaining strong relationships with other investors, professionals, and key players in the industry, you can gain access to better deals, insights, and opportunities that would otherwise be unavailable. Whether you attend local events, engage on social media, or form strategic partnerships, networking helps expand your influence, increase your knowledge, and accelerate your success in real estate investing. Take the time to build a network of trusted connections, and your real estate investment business will thrive.

Real Estate Investment Trusts (REITs)

For those who are interested in real estate investing but are not yet ready to buy property directly, Real Estate Investment Trusts (REITs) offer an excellent alternative. REITs allow investors to invest in large-scale, income-producing real estate without the complexities of owning or managing property themselves. In this chapter, we will explore how REITs work, the different types available, and the potential benefits they offer to investors.

1. What is a Real Estate Investment Trust (REIT)?

A Real Estate Investment Trust (REIT) is a company that owns, operates, or finances real estate that generates income. The primary goal of a REIT is to provide investors with an opportunity to invest in large, income-generating properties without directly owning or managing them. REITs typically focus on specific types of real estate, such as residential, commercial, or industrial properties, and they make investments that are designed to yield income through rental payments, interest on mortgages, or property sales.

REAL ESTATE INVESTMENT TRUSTS (REITS)

REITs are similar to mutual funds in that they pool money from multiple investors to buy, manage, and sell real estate. They are also traded on major stock exchanges, much like stocks or bonds. This means that, as an investor, you can buy shares of a REIT on the stock market, gaining exposure to real estate investments with the liquidity and flexibility of a traditional stock investment.

2. How Do REITs Work?

REITs pool investor capital to acquire and manage a portfolio of real estate assets. Once the capital is raised, the REIT uses it to buy properties that fit within its investment strategy. These properties are then managed by the REIT, and the income generated from them, such as rent payments or property sales, is distributed to the investors in the form of dividends.

Revenue Generation: The income from the properties is typically distributed in the form of regular dividends to investors, often on a quarterly or monthly basis. REITs are required by law to distribute at least 90% of their taxable income as dividends, which is why they tend to have high dividend yields.

Diversification: By investing in a REIT, you gain access to a diversified portfolio of properties. This diversification can help reduce risk by spreading your investment across multiple types of real estate, locations, and sectors.

Liquidity: Unlike direct property investments, REITs are traded on stock exchanges, meaning they offer liquidity. Investors can buy and sell shares in a REIT just like any other publicly traded stock. This makes REITs more accessible and flexible compared to owning physical real estate.

3. Types of REITs

There are several different types of REITs, each focusing on a specific area of the real estate market. The main types of REITs are:

a. Equity REITs

Equity REITs invest directly in and own income-generating real estate properties, such as office buildings, retail centers, apartments, and industrial facilities. The primary way they generate income is through the rent collected from these properties. Equity REITs typically focus on long-term investments and aim to generate steady, ongoing rental income.

Examples of properties: Office buildings, shopping malls, apartment complexes, hotels, warehouses.

Income generation: Rental income from tenants.

b. Mortgage REITs (mREITs)

Mortgage REITs, or mREITs, invest in real estate debt rather than physical properties. Instead of owning and managing buildings, mREITs provide financing for real estate projects by purchasing mortgages and mortgage-backed securities. The income generated by mREITs comes from the interest on the loans they make or the securities they hold.

Examples of assets: Residential and commercial mortgages, mortgage-backed securities.

Income generation: Interest income from the loans or securities they own.

c. Hybrid REITs

Hybrid REITs combine elements of both equity and mortgage REITs. They invest in a mix of physical real estate properties and real estate debt. Hybrid REITs provide a diversified investment strategy by offering exposure to both rental income and interest income.

Examples of assets: A portfolio that includes both properties and mortgage-backed securities.

Income generation: Both rental income and interest income.

d. Private REITs

Private REITs are not listed on public exchanges and are typically only available to institutional investors or accredited individuals. These REITs operate similarly to public REITs, but they may have different regulatory requirements and offer less liquidity.

Examples of assets: A variety of real estate types, depending on the REIT's strategy.

Income generation: Typically similar to public REITs but with different access and structure.

4. Benefits of Investing in REITs

Investing in REITs provides several key advantages for those looking to enter the real estate market without the hassle of managing property directly. Below are some of the primary benefits:

a. Access to Real Estate Markets

REITs allow individual investors to access high-quality, income-generating real estate that would otherwise be out of reach. For example, instead of buying a single office building or shopping center, you can invest in a REIT that holds a diversified portfolio of such assets, reducing individual exposure to risk.

b. High Dividend Yields

One of the most attractive aspects of REITs is their high dividend yields. Because they are required to distribute at least 90% of their taxable income as dividends, REITs often pay out significant portions of their income. This can provide investors with a steady stream of income, making them appealing for those seeking regular cash flow.

c. Diversification

Real estate can be a good way to diversify an investment portfolio, as it typically does not correlate directly with stock market movements. By adding REITs to your investment mix, you can reduce overall portfolio risk and potentially improve returns. Additionally, REITs give you access to a broad range of property sectors, such as residential, commercial, industrial, and healthcare real estate.

d. Liquidity

Since REITs are publicly traded on major stock exchanges, they offer liquidity that is not typically available with physical real estate investments. If you want to sell your investment in a property, it can take time to find a buyer and close the sale. With REITs, however, you can buy and sell shares easily, just like stocks, providing flexibility when managing your investment portfolio.

e. Tax Benefits

REITs benefit from special tax treatment under U.S. law, as long as they distribute the majority of their income as dividends. This means that they do not pay corporate taxes, which allows them to pass on more income to investors. Additionally, investors may be able to take advantage of tax-advantaged accounts, such as IRAs, to hold REITs and benefit from tax-deferred or tax-free growth.

5. Risks of Investing in REITs

While REITs offer numerous benefits, they also come with risks that investors should be aware of:

Market Risk: Like stocks, REITs are subject to market volatility. The price of REIT shares can fluctuate based on market conditions, interest rates, and broader economic factors.

Interest Rate Sensitivity: REITs, especially mortgage REITs, can be sensitive to changes in interest rates. Rising rates can negatively impact the value of their underlying assets and the profitability of their investments.

Sector-Specific Risks: Some REITs are concentrated in a specific sector (e.g., commercial real estate or healthcare facilities), meaning they may be more vulnerable to downturns in that sector.

Liquidity Risks (Private REITs): Private REITs are not as liquid as publicly traded ones, which can make it harder to sell your investment if needed.

6. How to Invest in REITs

Investing in REITs is straightforward, especially for those familiar with stock market investing. Here's how to get started:

REAL ESTATE INVESTMENT TRUSTS (REITS)

1. Choose Your REITs: Research different types of REITs and choose the one(s) that align with your investment goals and risk tolerance.

2. Buy Shares: You can purchase shares of publicly traded REITs through brokerage accounts, just like any other stock. If you're investing in private REITs, you may need to go through a private placement or an accredited investment platform.

3. Monitor Performance: Once you've invested in REITs, it's important to track their performance, including dividends, stock price movements, and any changes in the underlying properties or sectors.

Real Estate Investment Trusts (REITs) offer a unique and accessible way for investors to gain exposure to real estate without the complexities of owning physical property. Whether you're looking for regular income through dividends, diversification for your portfolio, or exposure to high-quality real estate assets, REITs provide an attractive alternative to direct property ownership. As with any investment, it's important to understand the risks involved, but for many, REITs offer an easy, efficient, and effective way to invest in real estate.

Risk Management in Real Estate

Real estate investing, like any form of investment, involves risks. However, by implementing effective risk management strategies, you can minimize potential losses and safeguard your investments. This chapter will guide you through the process of assessing and managing risks in real estate, focusing on the importance of insurance, diversification, and setting realistic expectations.

1. Understanding Real Estate Risk

Real estate investment risks come in many forms, from market fluctuations to unexpected property damages. The key to success is learning to identify these risks and develop strategies to manage them. Common types of risks in real estate include:

Market Risk: The risk of declining property values due to changes in the economy, interest rates, or local market conditions.

Liquidity Risk: Real estate is generally illiquid, meaning it can take time to sell a property or access cash from an investment.

Operational Risk: Risks associated with the day-to-day management of properties, such as tenant issues, maintenance costs, or property vacancies.

Financing Risk: The possibility of rising interest rates or difficulty in securing financing that affects cash flow or returns.

Legal Risk: The potential for lawsuits or legal complications, including disputes with tenants or zoning issues.

2. Mitigating Risk through Insurance

Insurance is one of the most effective tools for managing risk in real estate investing. It provides financial protection against unforeseen events that could damage your property or disrupt your income. Some essential types of insurance include:

Property Insurance: Covers damage to your property from incidents like fire, theft, or natural disasters.

Liability Insurance: Protects you from lawsuits related to accidents that occur on your property, such as slip-and-fall incidents.

Loss of Income Insurance: Provides coverage in case your property becomes uninhabitable or rental income is disrupted due to damage.

Title Insurance: Protects against legal claims to your property's title, such as ownership disputes or unpaid liens.

Having the right insurance policies in place ensures that you can recover financially from unforeseen events and protect your assets from significant loss.

3. Diversification: Spreading Your Risk

Diversification is another crucial risk management strategy. By spreading your investments across different properties, markets, or types of real estate, you reduce the potential impact of any single risk. For example, if one property market declines, your other investments may remain unaffected.

Property Type Diversification: Consider investing in different property types (e.g., residential, commercial, industrial) to protect against market downturns in a specific sector.

Geographical Diversification: Spread your investments across different locations or cities. Local market conditions vary, and diversifying across regions can reduce the risk of being affected by a downturn in a single market.

Investment Vehicle Diversification: Explore different investment vehicles, such as Real Estate Investment Trusts (REITs), to balance risk and return without overexposing yourself to the volatility of direct property ownership.

Diversification helps you create a more resilient investment portfolio that can better weather economic downturns and market shifts.

4. Setting Realistic Expectations

Another essential element of risk management is setting realistic expectations for your investments. Unrealistic expectations can lead to poor decision-making, such as over-leveraging or overpaying for a property. Setting clear, achievable goals based on thorough market research and financial analysis is key to managing risk.

Understand Market Cycles: Real estate markets go through cycles of expansion and contraction. Knowing where the market is in its cycle can help you set more realistic expectations for property values and rental income.

Cash Flow Projections: Ensure that you have conservative cash flow projections in place. Account for vacancies, maintenance costs, and potential economic downturns when calculating your expected returns.

Plan for the Unexpected: Always budget for unexpected costs, such as repairs or tenant vacancies, to ensure your investments remain profitable even when things don't go as planned.

By setting realistic expectations and accounting for potential risks, you can avoid overextending yourself and mitigate the financial impact of adverse situations.

5. Using Leverage Wisely

While leverage can amplify returns, it can also increase risk.

Excessive debt can put you in a vulnerable position if property values drop or cash flow becomes disrupted. To manage this risk:

Avoid Over-Leveraging: Be mindful of your debt-to-equity ratio. Over-leveraging can lead to financial strain if market conditions worsen or if rental income does not meet expectations.

Refinance Strategically: If interest rates drop, refinancing your mortgage can help you lower your payments and reduce your financial exposure.

Stress Test Your Portfolio: Before using leverage, stress test your investments by considering worst-case scenarios. Calculate how your cash flow and debt obligations would be affected by a significant increase in interest rates or a property market downturn.

Using leverage responsibly can help you maximize returns while keeping risks in check.

6. Monitoring and Adapting to Changing Conditions

Risk management is an ongoing process. Market conditions, property values, and interest rates can change over time, and it's essential to continuously monitor your investments and adapt to these changes. Consider the following steps to stay on top of potential risks:

Regularly Review Your Portfolio: Assess your portfolio at least once a year to determine whether it's aligned with your risk tolerance and financial goals. Make adjustments as necessary.

Stay Informed: Keep up with industry trends, market shifts, and economic news. Being proactive about understanding the factors that influence real estate markets allows you to make informed decisions.

Reassess Your Insurance: As your portfolio grows, ensure that your insurance coverage evolves with it. Review your policies regularly to make sure you have adequate protection.

By staying vigilant and adapting your strategy based on changing conditions, you can better manage risk and protect your investments.

Risk management is an integral part of real estate investing. By using insurance, diversifying your investments, setting realistic expectations, and monitoring your portfolio, you can effectively mitigate the risks associated with real estate. With careful planning and strategic decision-making, you can build a more secure and profitable real estate investment portfolio, minimizing the potential for significant losses.

Negotiation Strategies for Real Estate Deals

Negotiation is one of the most crucial skills for real estate investors. Whether you're purchasing a property or selling one, the ability to negotiate effectively can significantly impact your profitability. In this chapter, we'll explore proven negotiation strategies that will help you secure the best deals, understand the art of persuasion, and avoid common pitfalls.

1. Understanding the Power of Negotiation

Real estate transactions often involve significant sums of money, making negotiation a powerful tool for both buyers and sellers. As an investor, your goal is to maximize your return on investment by negotiating favorable terms. Strong negotiation skills allow you to lower your purchase price, secure financing on better terms, or even gain additional benefits, such as repairs or credits, that can improve the overall deal.

In real estate, negotiations are not only about price. Terms like closing timelines, contingencies, and even seller concessions can be negotiated to your advantage.

2. Preparation: The Key to Successful Negotiations

The most successful negotiators are those who are prepared. Proper preparation will help you understand the property, the seller's motivation, and the market conditions, all of which are essential for negotiating effectively.

Do Your Homework: Research the property thoroughly. Know its market value, its history, and its condition. Understand the local real estate market trends, and be aware of any comparable sales (comps) in the area. The more knowledge you have, the better position you'll be in to negotiate.

Understand the Seller's Motivation: Sellers may have different reasons for selling, such as financial distress, relocation, or a desire to downsize. Understanding their motivations can help you determine how flexible they may be on price and terms.

Know Your Budget and Limits: Set clear boundaries for yourself. Know the maximum amount you're willing to pay and the terms you're willing to accept. It's essential to remain disciplined during the negotiation process to avoid overpaying for a property or agreeing to unfavorable terms.

3. The Art of Making an Offer

Your initial offer sets the tone for the entire negotiation process. A well-crafted offer shows that you're serious but also leaves room for negotiation. The following tips will help you make an effective offer:

Start Below Market Value: If you're confident in your research, it's usually best to start with an offer slightly below market value. This gives you room to negotiate upward while still landing on a favorable price.

Use Objective Data: Support your offer with facts, such as the condition of the property or comparable sales data. For example, if the property needs significant repairs or is overpriced compared to nearby properties, present that data to justify your lower offer.

Be Professional and Respectful: Even if you start with a low offer, approach the negotiation with respect and professionalism. A courteous and reasonable demeanor can help build rapport with the seller and make them more willing to engage in the process.

4. Negotiating Price and Terms

While price is often the primary concern in real estate negotiations, terms are equally important. Understanding how to negotiate both price and terms is essential for securing the best deal.

Focus on Win-Win Outcomes: Aim for a win-win situation where both parties feel satisfied. For example, if the seller is firm on price, see if they're open to negotiating other terms, such as the closing date or repair credits. This gives you more value without changing the price.

Leverage Timing: Timing can play a significant role in negotiations. If the seller is motivated to close quickly, you may be able to negotiate a better deal by offering a faster closing timeline. On the other hand, if you can be patient, you may be able to secure a better deal by waiting for the seller to become more flexible.

Use Contingencies to Your Advantage: Contingencies are conditions that must be met before the sale is finalized. Common contingencies include financing, inspections, and appraisals. Negotiating favorable contingencies can protect you if the deal doesn't go as planned.

5. Understanding the Seller's Position

To be an effective negotiator, you must understand the seller's position. This allows you to craft your negotiation strategy based on their needs and goals. Some sellers may be focused primarily on price, while others may care more about terms, such as the closing timeline.

Ask Questions: Don't be afraid to ask the seller why they're selling the property and what their ideal terms are. This information can help you tailor your offer and increase your chances of success.

Look for Leverage: If the seller is under financial pressure or has owned the property for a long time, they may be more motivated to accept a lower price or negotiate more flexible terms.

6. Negotiating Closing Costs and Other Seller Concessions

Closing costs are often a source of tension in real estate negotiations. Buyers and sellers may have different expectations about who should pay these costs. As a buyer, you can negotiate for the seller to cover some or all of the closing costs, which can help lower your overall expenses.

Seller Concessions: In a buyer's market or when the seller is motivated to close, you may be able to negotiate seller concessions. These may include the seller paying for part of the closing costs, providing a home warranty, or offering credits for repairs.

Splitting the Costs: If the seller is unwilling to cover all the costs, consider splitting them. Offering to cover part of the closing costs in exchange for a better price or additional repairs can be a win-win solution for both parties.

7. Negotiation Tactics to Avoid

While it's essential to be strategic in negotiations, it's equally important to avoid certain tactics that can backfire:

Being Too Aggressive: Aggressive or confrontational negotiating tactics can create tension and lead to a breakdown in negotiations. A cooperative, collaborative approach is usually more successful.

Making Too Many Concessions: While it's essential to be flexible, avoid giving in to every request from the seller. Overcommitting can erode your profits and weaken your negotiating position.

Rushing the Process: Take your time to understand the seller's motivations and needs before making any decisions. Rushing through the process may lead to costly mistakes.

8. Finalizing the Deal

Once you've agreed on price and terms, the final step is to finalize the deal. During this phase, review all documents carefully, including the purchase agreement, contingencies, and disclosures. It's essential to ensure that all the agreed-upon terms are written clearly in the contract before you sign.

Get Legal Advice: Always consult with an attorney or real estate agent to ensure that the contract protects your interests and is legally sound.

Stay Focused on Your Goals: Throughout the negotiation process, keep your financial goals and strategy in mind. Never lose sight of your investment objectives, even when faced with challenging negotiations.

Negotiation is an essential skill for any successful real estate investor. By preparing thoroughly, understanding the seller's position, and being flexible with price and terms, you can secure the best deals and maximize your profitability. Negotiating effectively requires patience, strategy, and a focus on creating win-win situations. Mastering these skills will set you apart in the competitive world of real estate investing.

Closing the Deal

After months of searching, negotiating, and preparing, you've finally secured a property. The next crucial step is closing the deal. The closing process can be complex and involves several key steps that, if not handled correctly, can delay or even derail your transaction. In this chapter, we will guide you through the closing process, covering everything from signing contracts to transferring ownership and handling closing costs.

1. Understanding the Closing Process

Closing is the final stage of the real estate transaction, where the property officially changes hands from the seller to the buyer. The goal is to complete all the necessary legal, financial, and administrative steps so that the property can be transferred to you, and you can take possession.

While the exact details of the closing process can vary depending on the jurisdiction and type of property, most real estate transactions follow a similar general procedure. Being prepared for each step of the process will ensure a smoother transaction and reduce the chances of surprises at the closing table.

2. Scheduling the Closing Date

Once both parties agree to the terms of the sale, the next step is scheduling the closing date. This is typically done once the seller has accepted your offer and you have completed necessary contingencies, such as inspections and appraisals.

Mutual Agreement: Both parties need to agree on the date of closing. The timeline often depends on the buyer's financing, the complexity of the deal, and the seller's availability.

Timeframe for Closing: Generally, closing occurs 30 to 60 days after the offer is accepted, but this can vary. If you're financing the purchase with a loan, the lender's approval process may also affect the timing.

3. Reviewing the Closing Disclosure

One of the most important documents you'll receive before closing is the Closing Disclosure. This document outlines the final details of your mortgage, including the loan terms, monthly payments, and the total amount you will pay over the life of the loan.

Timing: You must receive the Closing Disclosure at least three days before closing. This gives you time to review the details, ask questions, and resolve any discrepancies before the deal is finalized.

Details to Verify: Carefully check all the information listed in the document, including the loan amount, interest rate, closing costs, and monthly payments. Pay attention to any unexpected fees or changes from the initial estimate.

4. Reviewing and Signing the Contracts

At closing, you will be required to sign various legal documents, including the purchase agreement and the mortgage documents. These documents formalize the terms of the deal and transfer ownership of the property.

The Purchase Agreement: This is the main contract that outlines the price and terms of the sale. If any changes were made to the original agreement, such as repairs or price adjustments, those should be reflected in the final purchase agreement.

Mortgage Documents: If you are financing the property with a loan, you will need to sign the mortgage documents. These documents outline the terms of the loan, including the interest rate, repayment schedule, and the lender's rights in the event of default.

Title Transfer: In some jurisdictions, a separate deed transfer document must be signed to officially transfer ownership. This ensures that the seller's title to the property is legally passed to you.

5. Title Search and Title Insurance

One of the key aspects of closing is ensuring that the title to the property is clear. A title search is conducted to verify that the seller legally owns the property and there are no liens, disputes, or claims against it.

Title Search: This process checks for any unpaid property taxes, outstanding mortgages, or legal disputes related to the property. It ensures that there are no surprises after you take ownership.

Title Insurance: Title insurance protects you against any unforeseen title issues that may arise after the sale is completed. The cost of title insurance is usually a one-time fee, and it's generally recommended to purchase this insurance for peace of mind.

6. Dealing with Closing Costs

Closing costs are the fees associated with finalizing the sale of the property. These can include a range of expenses such as loan origination fees, appraisal fees, title insurance, and attorney fees.

Buyer's Closing Costs: As a buyer, you'll be responsible for paying various fees, including the down payment, lender fees, and title fees. Closing costs typically range from 2% to 5% of the purchase price, although this can vary based on the location and type of loan.

Seller's Closing Costs: The seller may also incur costs, including real estate agent commissions and any agreed-upon repairs or credits to the buyer. It's important to understand who is responsible for which costs during negotiations.

Negotiating Closing Costs: In some cases, the buyer and seller can negotiate who will cover certain closing costs. For example, the seller might agree to pay for some of the buyer's closing costs in exchange for a higher purchase price.

7. Final Walk-Through

Before officially closing, you will usually have the opportunity to conduct a final walk-through of the property. This is your chance to ensure that the property is in the same condition as it was when you agreed to buy it, and that any negotiated repairs or changes have been made.

What to Check: During the walk-through, verify that any agreed-upon repairs have been completed and that there are no new damages. Check that all appliances and systems are in working order.

Resolving Issues: If issues arise during the final walk-through, you can either request that they be resolved before closing or negotiate a credit at closing to cover the cost of repairs.

8. Closing Day

On the day of closing, you will meet with all parties involved, including the seller, their agent, your agent, the closing agent, and sometimes an attorney. This meeting is where the final documents are signed, funds are exchanged, and the property title is officially transferred to you.

Funding the Deal: On closing day, you will need to bring the funds required to close. This includes your down payment, closing costs, and any other fees. These funds are typically wired directly to the closing agent's account.

Receiving the Keys: Once the paperwork is signed and the transaction is complete, you will officially own the property. You will receive the keys, and the property will be transferred to you.

9. After Closing: Final Steps

Once the deal has closed, there are still a few important steps to take:

Record the Deed: In most jurisdictions, the deed to the property will be recorded with the county clerk or other local government office. This ensures that the property's transfer of ownership is officially documented in public records.

Review Your Documents: Keep all documents related to the transaction, including the purchase agreement, loan documents, and title insurance policy. These will be important for your records and for tax purposes.

Notify Relevant Parties: Make sure to notify your insurance company, utility companies, and local authorities of your change in address. If you're renting the property out, inform tenants about any changes.

Closing the deal is the final, and often the most complex, stage of the real estate investment process. From reviewing documents and signing contracts to paying closing costs and transferring ownership, each step requires careful attention to detail. By understanding the closing process, preparing for each phase, and staying organized, you can ensure a smooth and successful transaction. With the property officially in your name, you can move forward with your real estate investment journey, whether it's renting, flipping, or enjoying long-term appreciation.

Managing Your Property

Successfully managing your property is essential to ensuring it remains a profitable investment. Effective property management not only maximizes your rental income but also preserves the long-term value of your investment. In this chapter, we'll explore key practices for managing your property, from tenant screening to ongoing maintenance.

1. Tenant Screening

The tenants you choose can make or break your rental investment. Proper tenant screening helps ensure that your tenants will pay rent on time and take care of the property. A thorough screening process includes:

Background Checks: Verify tenants' criminal background and eviction history. This step helps avoid problematic tenants who may cause trouble or fail to pay rent.

Credit Checks: A credit check helps determine the financial responsibility of potential tenants. Look for applicants with good credit scores to minimize the risk of late payments.

Income Verification: Ensure that tenants have a steady income that is sufficient to cover the rent. Generally, their monthly income should be at least three times the rent amount.

References: Contact previous landlords to verify tenants' rental history. Positive references indicate a tenant who is likely to respect your property and pay rent on time.

2. Setting Rent Prices

Setting the right rent price is key to attracting quality tenants while ensuring you cover your expenses and generate a profit. Consider the following factors when determining your rent:

Market Research: Research comparable properties in your area to see what similar rentals are charging. Price your property competitively based on location, size, and amenities.

Costs and Profit Margin: Ensure the rent you charge covers your mortgage payments, property taxes, insurance, and maintenance costs, while also providing a reasonable return on your investment.

Rent Increases: Be mindful of market conditions and rent control laws in your area when increasing rent. Providing a fair increase can help retain good tenants while keeping your property profitable.

3. Lease Agreements

A well-drafted lease agreement is crucial to protect both you and your tenants. The lease should outline the terms of the rental agreement, including:

Duration of Lease: Specify the length of the lease (e.g., one year) and the renewal process.

Payment Terms: Outline rent payment deadlines, methods of payment, and penalties for late payments.

Responsibilities and Expectations: Clarify tenants' responsibilities for paying utilities, maintaining the property, and following community rules.

Termination Clause: Include details about the process for ending the lease, whether it's for non-payment or at the tenant's request.

4. Property Maintenance

Regular maintenance is critical to keep the property in good condition and retain tenants. Here are some tips for efficient property upkeep:

Routine Inspections: Conduct regular inspections to check for damage and ensure that tenants are maintaining the property properly. Set a schedule for these inspections, but always provide notice to tenants.

Repairs and Upgrades: Address any maintenance issues promptly to prevent small problems from turning into costly repairs. Regularly invest in upgrades that enhance the property's value, such as new appliances or fresh paint.

Preventive Maintenance: Perform regular tasks like changing air filters, cleaning gutters, and servicing HVAC systems to prevent larger issues. A well-maintained property is more attractive to tenants and can reduce long-term costs.

5. Handling Tenant Issues

Even with thorough screening and regular maintenance, tenant issues can arise. Having a plan for handling problems can help you resolve conflicts smoothly and keep tenants satisfied. Key strategies include:

Communication: Foster open and respectful communication with tenants. Address concerns promptly and professionally to maintain a positive relationship.

Dispute Resolution: If conflicts arise (e.g., noise complaints, maintenance disputes), try to resolve them amicably before they escalate. Consider setting clear boundaries and addressing issues in the lease agreement.

Evictions: While evictions are a last resort, it's important to understand the legal process in your area. Always follow the proper legal steps to avoid potential lawsuits.

6. Accounting and Recordkeeping

Proper financial management is crucial for maximizing the profitability of your investment. Keep accurate records of all income and expenses, including:

Rent Payments: Track when rent is paid and when it's late. This helps you identify any payment issues and take action if necessary.

Expenses: Keep track of all property-related expenses, including maintenance, utilities, insurance, and property management fees. This helps when filing taxes and tracking the profitability of your investment.

Tax Deductions: Real estate investors can deduct many expenses, including mortgage interest, property management fees, and depreciation. Keeping accurate records will help maximize your tax benefits.

7. Hiring Property Management Help

If managing a property becomes overwhelming, or if you own multiple properties, hiring a property management company can be an effective solution. Property managers handle tasks like tenant screening, rent collection, maintenance, and legal issues. While you will need to pay a fee (typically 8-12% of the rent), a property manager can save you time and reduce the stress of managing a rental property yourself.

Selecting a Property Manager: When choosing a property management company, look for experience, good references, and a clear understanding of local rental laws. Make sure the terms of their services align with your investment goals.

8. Building Long-Term Relationships with Tenants

Retaining tenants over the long term is beneficial for maintaining consistent cash flow and reducing turnover costs. Here are a few strategies for building lasting relationships:

Prompt Repairs: Always address repair requests quickly to demonstrate that you care about the property and your tenants' needs.

Respect Privacy: Respect your tenants' privacy by giving adequate notice before entering the property and communicating clearly about any upcoming inspections or repairs.

Create a Positive Environment: Make the property a pleasant place to live by ensuring safety, cleanliness, and a sense of community. Happy tenants are more likely to stay and take care of the property.

9. Legal and Regulatory Compliance

Real estate investing comes with its fair share of legal responsibilities. Make sure you are complying with all local laws and regulations, including:

Fair Housing Laws: Ensure your rental practices are non-discriminatory and comply with federal and state fair housing laws.

Tenant Rights: Familiarize yourself with tenants' rights in your jurisdiction to avoid legal disputes. This includes rules about security deposits, eviction procedures, and tenant privacy.

Building Codes and Permits: Make sure all repairs and renovations are up to code and that you obtain any necessary permits for work done on the property.

Effective property management is a critical component of successful real estate investing. By screening tenants carefully, maintaining your property, handling issues promptly, and managing finances efficiently, you can ensure that your investment remains profitable. Whether you choose to manage the property yourself or hire a property management company, adopting best practices in property management will set you up for long-term success.

Using Technology in Real Estate Investing

The digital age has fundamentally transformed the way we invest in real estate. With a multitude of tools and platforms at your disposal, technology can enhance every aspect of your investment journey, from property search and market analysis to managing your properties and finances. In this chapter, we'll explore how technology can help streamline the investing process, providing you with the tools you need to make smarter decisions and increase your efficiency.

1. Property Search Engines

Gone are the days of relying solely on real estate agents and local newspapers for property listings. Property search engines have become one of the most powerful tools in real estate investing. Websites like Zillow, Realtor.com, and Redfin allow you to search for properties across various markets, helping you quickly find potential investments.

Benefits of Property Search Engines:

Wide Reach: Access listings from across the country or even globally, helping you find deals in emerging markets.

Filter Options: Narrow down your search using filters for price, location, property type, and other criteria, making it easier to find properties that meet your investment goals.

Market Insights: Many platforms offer market trends, historical pricing data, and neighborhood statistics, which can be invaluable for evaluating the potential of a property.

2. Investment Calculators

Real estate investment calculators are invaluable for evaluating the financial viability of a potential property. These tools allow you to quickly assess key metrics such as cash flow, return on investment (ROI), cap rates, and more. With the right investment calculator, you can determine if a property will provide a good return before even making an offer.

Types of Investment Calculators:

Cash Flow Calculators: Calculate the monthly income you can expect from a rental property after factoring in expenses like mortgage payments, property taxes, and maintenance costs.

Cap Rate Calculators: Measure the profitability of a property by dividing the net operating income (NOI) by the property's purchase price.

ROI Calculators: Assess the overall return on investment, factoring in property appreciation, tax benefits, and other financial aspects.

Using these calculators ensures you're making data-driven decisions and can help you avoid emotional or impulsive purchases.

3. Real Estate Management Software

As your real estate portfolio grows, keeping track of your properties, finances, and tenants can become overwhelming. Real estate management software provides a comprehensive solution to streamline these tasks, offering features such as online rent collection, maintenance tracking, and financial reporting. Popular software includes AppFolio, Buildium, and TenantCloud.

Benefits of Real Estate Management Software:

Automation: Automate tasks such as rent collection, late fee notices, and lease renewals, saving you time and reducing human error.

Financial Management: Track income and expenses, generate profit and loss reports, and maintain detailed financial records for tax purposes.

Tenant Communication: Many platforms offer tenant portals

where tenants can pay rent, submit maintenance requests, and communicate with you directly, improving tenant satisfaction and making management more efficient.

4. Market Analysis Tools

In today's fast-paced real estate market, staying informed about trends and market conditions is essential. Technology has made market analysis easier and more comprehensive than ever before. Tools like Mashvisor, PropStream, and NeighborhoodScout provide in-depth analysis of property values, rental income potential, and even neighborhood-level data to help investors make informed decisions.

What You Can Analyze:

Neighborhood Trends: Gain insight into job growth, population shifts, and future development plans that could influence property values.

Comparable Sales: Easily find comparable property sales to assess whether a property is priced competitively or if there is room for negotiation.

Rental Demand: Analyze rental income potential and occupancy rates to gauge whether a property will generate steady cash flow.

5. Virtual Tours and Augmented Reality (AR)

Virtual tours and augmented reality (AR) tools have revolutionized property viewing, especially in today's digital-first environment. Platforms like Matterport and Zillow 3D allow potential buyers and renters to explore properties remotely, providing a more interactive experience than traditional photos.

Benefits of Virtual Tours and AR:

Time-Saving: You can quickly view and evaluate multiple properties without the need to visit them in person, making the decision process faster and more efficient.

Improved Visualization: Virtual tours provide a 360-degree view of the property, helping you visualize how the space could be used or renovated.

Remote Investment: These tools allow you to invest in properties outside your immediate area without having to travel, opening up new markets.

6. Blockchain and Smart Contracts

Blockchain technology is beginning to play a role in real estate investing, offering a more secure and transparent way to handle transactions. Blockchain enables the use of smart contracts, which are digital agreements that automatically execute when certain conditions are met. This technology can help reduce paperwork, speed up the transaction process, and enhance security.

Benefits of Blockchain and Smart Contracts:

Transparency: Blockchain ensures that all parties have access to the same information, reducing the chances of fraud or disputes.

Efficiency: Smart contracts eliminate the need for intermediaries, making the transaction process faster and more efficient.

Security: Blockchain provides a secure and tamper-proof way to store contracts and transaction details.

7. Crowdfunding Platforms

Real estate crowdfunding platforms such as Fundrise, RealtyMogul, and Crowdstreet offer a way to invest in real estate without directly owning property. These platforms pool money from multiple investors to fund real estate projects, allowing you to invest in commercial or residential properties with relatively small capital.

Benefits of Real Estate Crowdfunding:

Lower Entry Barriers: Crowdfunding allows you to invest in real estate with a lower initial investment than purchasing properties directly.

Diversification: By pooling funds with other investors, you can diversify your real estate investments across multiple properties or projects.

Passive Investment: Crowdfunding is a hands-off investment strategy, where the platform manages the property, and you receive returns from the rental income or sale.

8. AI and Predictive Analytics

Artificial intelligence (AI) and predictive analytics tools are becoming more advanced in real estate investing. These technologies can analyze large sets of data to predict future property values, market trends, and even the best times to buy or sell.

How AI Helps Real Estate Investors:

Property Valuation: AI algorithms can provide more accurate property valuations by analyzing historical data and current market conditions.

Trend Forecasting: Predictive analytics can identify emerging markets and areas that are likely to experience property appreciation in the future.

Risk Assessment: AI can help assess potential risks associated with a property or investment strategy, making it easier to make data-driven decisions.

9. Social Media and Digital Marketing

Using social media and digital marketing tools can help you reach a wider audience when buying or selling properties. Platforms like Facebook, Instagram, LinkedIn, and YouTube allow you to promote properties, network with other investors, and build your brand as a real estate professional.

Benefits of Social Media in Real Estate:

Brand Awareness: Use social media to share your success stories, investment tips, and market insights to build your reputation as a knowledgeable investor.

Property Promotion: Showcase your properties with photos, videos, and virtual tours to attract potential buyers or renters.

Networking Opportunities: Connect with other investors, agents, and industry professionals to expand your network and gain access to off-market deals.

Technology has opened up new possibilities in real estate

investing, making it easier to research, analyze, and manage investments. From property search engines and investment calculators to virtual tours and blockchain technology, these tools help streamline the process, saving you time and money. By leveraging the power of technology, you can make smarter investment decisions, increase efficiency, and ultimately achieve greater success in the real estate market.

Scaling Your Real Estate Portfolio

After successfully completing your first investment, scaling your real estate portfolio is the natural next step to building long-term wealth. Growing your portfolio involves strategic planning, increasing your access to capital, and managing a wider variety of properties. In this chapter, we'll explore key strategies to help you scale your real estate investments efficiently and sustainably.

1. Diversify Into Different Property Types

One of the most effective ways to scale your portfolio is by diversifying across various property types. While single-family homes and multi-family units are popular choices, exploring commercial real estate, vacation rentals, or industrial properties can yield higher returns and reduce risk.

Benefits of Diversification:

Risk Mitigation: Different property types respond to market changes in unique ways. For example, residential properties might perform well during a downturn while industrial properties may remain stable.

Income Streams: Diversification creates multiple revenue streams, including rental income from apartments, commercial leases, or short-term rentals, allowing you to stabilize cash flow.

Access to New Markets: Investing in various property types can open doors to emerging markets or more lucrative areas where demand is high.

2. Leverage Other People's Capital (OPM)

As you scale, using other people's capital (OPM) becomes a powerful tool to expand your portfolio without using your own funds for every deal. OPM can come in the form of loans, partnerships, or private investors who are willing to fund your acquisitions.

Ways to Leverage OPM:

Conventional Loans: As your portfolio grows, banks and lenders may offer you better terms due to your established track record.

Private Investors: You can partner with individuals or groups who are willing to invest in your projects in exchange for equity, fixed returns, or a share of the profits.

Real Estate Syndications: Pooling funds with other investors allows you to take on larger projects, such as commercial properties or apartment complexes, that might otherwise be out of reach.

3. Use Refinancing to Unlock Capital

Refinancing your properties is a common strategy used to free up capital for further investments. By leveraging the equity in your existing properties, you can secure better loan terms, lower interest rates, or pull cash out to fund additional acquisitions.

Refinancing Strategies:

Cash-Out Refinance: This allows you to borrow against the equity in your property, turning that equity into cash to invest in new deals.

Rate and Term Refinance: Refinancing to a better rate can reduce your monthly payments, freeing up more cash flow for reinvestment.

HELOC (Home Equity Line of Credit): A HELOC provides access to capital based on the equity in your property, offering flexibility to withdraw funds when needed.

4. Invest in Larger Properties

As your portfolio grows, you can transition from smaller residential properties to larger, more profitable investments. Multi-family units, commercial buildings, and mixed-use developments often provide higher returns and greater economies of scale.

Benefits of Investing in Larger Properties:

Increased Cash Flow: Larger properties often generate more income, helping to rapidly accelerate the growth of your portfolio.

Economies of Scale: Managing multiple units in a single building can be more cost-effective than managing several smaller properties spread out across various locations.

Attractive to Institutional Investors: Larger properties may attract institutional investors, providing additional opportunities for joint ventures or selling your properties for significant profits.

5. Implement Property Management Systems

As your portfolio expands, managing multiple properties can become overwhelming without the proper systems in place. Property management software and delegating responsibilities to a professional team can streamline your operations.

Efficient Property Management:

Outsource to Professionals: As you scale, consider hiring a property management company to handle day-to-day operations, tenant relations, and maintenance tasks.

Use Technology: Invest in property management software to automate tasks such as rent collection, lease management, and financial tracking.

Set Systems for Maintenance and Repairs: Having a reliable system for handling property maintenance requests can help ensure that your investments stay in good condition and tenant turnover is minimized.

6. Increase Operational Efficiency

The larger your portfolio, the more important it becomes to optimize operational efficiency. By reviewing and improving processes related to finance, property management, and tenant relations, you can minimize expenses and maximize profits.

Ways to Increase Efficiency:

Streamline Financials: Set up systems for easy accounting, budgeting, and financial reporting across your portfolio.

Centralize Vendor Relationships: Build strong relationships with contractors, vendors, and suppliers to ensure quicker response times and better deals.

Enhance Tenant Retention: Focusing on tenant satisfaction through consistent communication, timely maintenance, and incentives for long-term leases can help reduce turnover and ensure steady cash flow.

7. Automate Reinvestment Strategies

A key to scaling is reinvesting your profits strategically to continue building your portfolio. Automating your reinvestment strategy through a clear financial plan ensures you're consistently growing while maintaining a strong cash flow.

Automated Reinvestment Tactics:

Set a Percentage for Reinvestment: Allocate a set percentage of your profits for reinvestment into new properties or property improvements.

Use a Profit-Led Growth Model: Focus on expanding your portfolio based on your profits, ensuring that you have the financial backing for each new investment.

Reinvest in High-Return Properties: Identify the properties that generate the highest returns and prioritize reinvestment in these areas.

8. Maintain a Balanced Debt-to-Equity Ratio

While leveraging other people's capital can fuel growth, it's important to manage your debt-to-equity ratio to avoid over-leveraging. Keeping a balanced approach to borrowing ensures that you're not exposing yourself to unnecessary risk.

Managing Debt-to-Equity Ratio:

Evaluate Borrowing Capacity: Before taking on additional debt, assess your current financial situation to ensure you can comfortably service new loans.

Diversify Financing Sources: Use a mix of loans, investor funds, and personal savings to fund your deals without over-relying on one source of capital.

Build Equity: As your portfolio grows, focus on increasing equity by paying down debt or investing in properties with strong appreciation potential.

9. Focus on Long-Term Growth

Scaling your real estate portfolio is a marathon, not a sprint. As you acquire more properties, stay focused on long-term growth rather than short-term profits. This approach will ensure your investments continue to appreciate, and you build a legacy for future generations.

Long-Term Growth Strategies:

Hold Properties for Appreciation: While flipping can be profitable, holding onto properties for long-term appreciation ensures steady wealth-building.

Consider Estate Planning: As you scale, start thinking about how your properties fit into your long-term financial and estate planning goals.

Expand Into New Markets: Look beyond your current market to diversify and tap into growing areas that will offer higher returns over time.

Scaling your real estate portfolio requires careful planning, access to capital, and strategic diversification. By leveraging OPM, diversifying property types, implementing efficient management systems, and focusing on long-term growth, you can grow your investments exponentially. Keep refining your processes, building a strong network, and using available tools to maximize your potential for success as your real estate journey continues to evolve.

Managing Cash Flow and Profits

Effective cash flow management is essential for the success and sustainability of any real estate investment. Whether you're dealing with rental properties or flipping homes, understanding how to manage your cash flow ensures that your investments remain profitable. In this chapter, we'll explore strategies for tracking income and expenses, maintaining a healthy cash flow, and reinvesting profits to maximize returns.

1. Understanding Cash Flow in Real Estate

Cash flow refers to the money that comes in and goes out of your property investments. A positive cash flow means your income exceeds your expenses, while a negative cash flow indicates you're losing money. Managing this flow is vital for sustaining and growing your portfolio.

Key Cash Flow Components:

Rental Income: The primary income stream from rental properties. This includes monthly rent payments made by tenants.

Expenses: Costs such as property taxes, insurance, maintenance, utilities, mortgage payments, and property management fees.

Net Cash Flow: The difference between your total income and expenses. A positive net cash flow means the property is earning money, while a negative net cash flow may indicate potential problems.

2. Tracking Income and Expenses

To effectively manage cash flow, it's crucial to track all sources of income and every expense associated with your property investments. Accurate tracking helps ensure that you stay on top of your finances, identify areas where you can cut costs, and make informed decisions.

Income Tracking:

Record all rental payments, including regular and late payments. Use property management software or spreadsheets to stay organized.

Track any additional income from the property, such as parking fees, laundry services, or late-payment penalties.

Expense Tracking:

Regularly monitor expenses, including repairs, maintenance, and utilities. Keeping an eye on these costs ensures you don't overspend.

Create a budget for each property to predict and manage both fixed and variable expenses. A detailed budget can help you spot potential issues before they become expensive problems.

3. Building and Maintaining a Cash Reserve

Unexpected expenses are part of real estate investing. From emergency repairs to vacancies, having a cash reserve is crucial to maintaining financial stability. A well-funded reserve allows you to cover these costs without relying on loans or disrupting your investment strategy.

How to Build a Cash Reserve:

Set aside a portion of your rental income each month into a separate reserve fund.

Determine an appropriate reserve size, typically 3-6 months of property expenses, to cover major repairs, vacancies, or other unforeseen events.

Avoid using this fund for non-emergency expenses to ensure it's available when needed.

4. Reinvesting Profits for Growth

Reinvesting profits is a key strategy for scaling your real estate portfolio. Instead of spending the cash flow, using it to acquire more properties or fund property improvements can significantly increase long-term returns.

Reinvestment Options:

Acquiring More Properties: Use the profits from existing properties to fund down payments on new acquisitions, expanding your portfolio.

Property Upgrades: Invest in renovations or upgrades that can increase the property's value and rental income, leading to higher long-term profitability.

Debt Reduction: Use cash flow to pay down debt on properties, which reduces your interest expenses and increases your equity.

5. Maximizing Profits with Tax Strategies

Understanding how taxes impact your cash flow and profits is essential for real estate investors. By utilizing tax strategies, you can minimize your tax burden and keep more of your earnings.

Depreciation: Real estate properties are eligible for depreciation, which can offset income and reduce your taxable profits.

1031 Exchange: A tax-deferred exchange allows you to defer paying capital gains taxes on the sale of a property if you reinvest the proceeds in a like-kind property.

Deductions: Deductible expenses such as property management fees, insurance, and repairs can reduce your taxable income, leading to lower taxes and increased profits.

6. Handling Vacancies and Late Payments

Vacancies and late payments can significantly impact cash flow. To minimize these disruptions, it's important to have systems in place for screening tenants, setting clear payment terms, and responding to issues promptly.

Tenant Screening: Conduct thorough background and credit checks to ensure tenants are financially responsible and likely to pay on time.

Late Payment Policies: Implement clear policies for late payments, including grace periods and penalties. Ensure that tenants are aware of these policies upfront.

Minimize Vacancies: Keep your properties well-maintained to attract quality tenants. Additionally, staying ahead of lease expiration dates and marketing early can help minimize vacancy periods.

7. Tracking Key Metrics for Cash Flow

To gain a comprehensive understanding of your property's financial health, regularly track key metrics that indicate whether your cash flow is sustainable and growing.

Cash-on-Cash Return: This metric measures the return on your investment based on the actual cash invested, not the total value of the property. A high cash-on-cash return indicates strong cash flow relative to the amount of money you've invested.

Cap Rate (Capitalization Rate): The cap rate measures the profitability of a property by comparing its annual net operating income to its purchase price. A higher cap rate typically indicates better cash flow potential.

Debt Service Coverage Ratio (DSCR): This ratio compares your property's net operating income to its debt payments. A DSCR greater than 1 indicates that your property generates enough income to cover debt obligations.

8. Using Technology to Manage Cash Flow

Leverage technology to simplify cash flow management and gain real-time insights into your finances. Property management software, accounting tools, and financial apps can help you track income and expenses, automate payments, and analyze your financial performance.

Property Management Software: Many platforms offer built-in financial tracking features that allow you to monitor rent payments, expenses, and overall cash flow in one place.

Accounting Tools: Integrate accounting tools to automate tax calculations, generate financial reports, and track deductions.

Financial Apps: Use mobile apps to track your spending, monitor your reserve fund, and analyze your portfolio's performance.

9. Monitoring Long-Term Cash Flow Sustainability

Managing cash flow isn't just about tracking monthly income and expenses. It's also about assessing the long-term sustainability of your cash flow strategy. Regularly review your properties' financial performance and make adjustments as needed.

Review Performance Regularly: Conduct quarterly or annual reviews of your properties to assess their cash flow and overall profitability.

Adjust Strategies: If a property isn't generating the expected cash flow, consider adjusting rental rates, making improvements, or even selling it to reinvest in more profitable assets.

Plan for the Future: As you grow your portfolio, anticipate future expenses such as maintenance, capital expenditures, and property taxes. Planning ahead ensures that you're prepared to manage cash flow in the long term.

Managing cash flow and profits is at the core of successful real estate investing. By tracking income and expenses, maintaining a cash reserve, reinvesting profits, utilizing tax strategies, and using technology, you can ensure your investments remain profitable and continue to grow. A well-managed cash flow strategy allows you to maximize returns, reduce financial stress, and scale your real estate portfolio effectively over time.

Avoiding Common Real Estate Mistakes

Real estate investing can be a lucrative endeavor, but it's also filled with pitfalls, especially for beginners. Many first-time investors make mistakes that can derail their progress and lead to costly consequences. In this chapter, we'll highlight some of the most common mistakes made by new real estate investors and provide practical tips on how to avoid them.

1. Failing to Do Proper Research

One of the most costly mistakes beginners make is jumping into investments without thoroughly researching the market and the property. Inadequate research can lead to poor decisions that affect the long-term profitability of an investment.

How to Avoid It:

Study local market trends, property values, and rental demand.

Analyze the neighborhood's safety, amenities, and future

development plans.

Use tools like MLS listings, market reports, and property valuation sites to gather data.

2. Overestimating Rental Income and Underestimating Expenses

New investors often overestimate how much they can charge for rent while underestimating their monthly expenses. This can result in properties that are not cash-flow positive, leading to financial strain.

How to Avoid It:

Research comparable rental properties in the area to get an accurate idea of rental income potential.

Carefully calculate all property expenses, including taxes, insurance, maintenance, and property management fees, to get a true picture of profitability.

3. Ignoring the Importance of Location

Location is one of the most critical factors in determining a property's value and rental income potential. New investors sometimes focus too much on property features or price and neglect the surrounding area, which can lead to poor investment outcomes.

How to Avoid It:

Invest in properties located in areas with strong job growth, good schools, and low crime rates.

Look for neighborhoods with rising demand, which can lead to appreciation in property values.

4. Overleveraging and Taking on Too Much Debt

Many beginners use excessive leverage, borrowing more than they can handle to finance their investments. While leverage can amplify returns, it also increases risk, especially if property values drop or rental income doesn't meet expectations.

How to Avoid It:

Avoid overextending yourself financially by keeping your debt-to-income ratio in check.

Focus on properties that you can afford to manage with a reasonable amount of leverage.

5. Neglecting Property Maintenance

Neglecting property maintenance is a mistake that can lead to costly repairs and decreased property value. Failing to address small issues early can cause bigger, more expensive problems down the road.

How to Avoid It:

Regularly inspect properties and keep up with necessary maintenance.

Budget for repairs and maintenance costs, and consider setting up a reserve fund for unexpected expenses.

6. Being Emotionally Attached to the Property

Real estate is an investment, not an emotional purchase. Many new investors fall in love with a property, even when it doesn't meet their investment criteria. This emotional attachment can cloud judgment and lead to poor financial decisions.

How to Avoid It:

Evaluate properties objectively, focusing on their potential for returns rather than personal feelings.

Stick to your investment strategy and don't let emotions dictate your decisions.

7. Underestimating the Time and Effort Required

Real estate investing requires time, effort, and attention to detail. Many new investors underestimate the amount of work needed to manage properties, handle tenants, and stay on top of market trends.

How to Avoid It:

Be realistic about the time commitment required to manage your investments.

Consider hiring property managers or leveraging technology to streamline operations if necessary.

8. Lack of a Clear Exit Strategy

Without a clear exit strategy, investors may find themselves stuck with properties that aren't profitable or that no longer align with their financial goals. Having an exit plan is essential to know when to sell or move on to a different investment.

How to Avoid It:

Establish your long-term goals and define your exit strategy early on.

Decide whether you want to hold the property for long-term appreciation, flip it for a quick profit, or sell if it no longer meets your investment objectives.

9. Ignoring Legal and Tax Implications

Real estate investments have legal and tax implications that must be understood to avoid costly mistakes. Beginners sometimes overlook the legalities of contracts, zoning laws, and taxes, which can lead to fines, penalties, and other issues.

How to Avoid It:

Consult with a real estate attorney to review contracts and ensure compliance with local laws.

Understand the tax implications of your investments and seek advice from a tax professional to optimize deductions and minimize liabilities.

10. Not Having Enough Liquidity

Real estate investments often require substantial upfront capital, but they can also come with unexpected expenses that need to be covered immediately. Not having enough liquidity to cover these costs can result in financial strain or forced sales at a loss.

How to Avoid It:

Maintain a liquidity cushion to cover emergencies, repairs, vacancies, and other unforeseen expenses.

Ensure that you have enough cash flow or access to credit to handle property-related costs.

11. Not Diversifying Your Portfolio

Putting all your money into one property or one type of real estate investment can be risky. A lack of diversification increases your vulnerability to market downturns and unexpected challenges.

How to Avoid It:

Diversify your investments across different property types (residential, commercial, multifamily, etc.) and locations to spread risk.

Consider alternative investments like REITs or crowdfunding platforms to further diversify your portfolio.

12. Being Impatient

Real estate is typically a long-term investment. New investors may become impatient when returns don't materialize quickly and may make hasty decisions, such as selling too soon or making unnecessary changes to the property.

How to Avoid It:

Understand that real estate investments take time to yield substantial returns.

Stick to your investment plan, and be patient while allowing the property to appreciate or generate rental income over time.

Avoiding these common mistakes can help you set yourself up for success in real estate investing. By doing your research, maintaining financial discipline, and being strategic in your decision-making, you can build a strong foundation for your real estate portfolio. Keep learning, stay patient, and always remember that experience will be your best teacher in the world of real estate investing.

Moving Forward and Staying Motivated

Real estate investing is not a get-rich-quick endeavor. It's a long-term journey that requires patience, discipline, and a continuous willingness to learn. In this final chapter, we'll discuss how to stay motivated, remain focused on your goals, and keep growing your investment portfolio over time.

1. Set Clear, Achievable Goals

One of the best ways to stay motivated is by setting clear, measurable, and achievable goals. Whether you aim to acquire a certain number of properties within a year or achieve a specific return on investment, having concrete objectives keeps you focused and on track.

How to Stay on Track:

Break down your long-term goals into smaller, manageable steps.

Celebrate small wins, like securing your first property or achieving a positive cash flow.

2. Embrace Continuous Learning

The real estate market is constantly changing. To stay ahead of the curve, commit to lifelong learning. Whether it's through books, podcasts, seminars, or networking with other investors, the more knowledge you gain, the more confident and capable you'll become.

How to Stay Updated:

Stay informed about market trends, new technologies, and changes in regulations.

Attend real estate events and connect with experienced investors to gain new insights.

3. Adapt and Evolve Your Strategy

As your experience grows, your strategy should evolve. Don't be afraid to adapt to new market conditions or shift your focus when necessary. For example, if the rental market is weak, consider pivoting to flipping houses, or explore emerging markets that offer better opportunities.

How to Adapt:

Analyze what's working and what isn't in your current strategy.

Be flexible and open to exploring different investment types, like REITs, commercial properties, or crowdfunding.

4. Manage Your Expectations

Real estate investing can be full of ups and downs. Not every deal will be a home run, and there will be setbacks along the way. It's important to manage your expectations and understand that it takes time to build a successful portfolio.

How to Stay Resilient:

Keep the bigger picture in mind. Real estate is a long-term investment, and not every property will give immediate returns.

Learn from your mistakes and use them as stepping stones to future success.

5. Create a Support System

Real estate investing can sometimes feel isolating, especially if you're navigating it alone. Surround yourself with a network of like-minded individuals who can offer support, guidance, and encouragement.

How to Build a Network:

Join real estate groups, online forums, or local meetups where you can share experiences and advice.

Seek out mentors who have been through the ups and downs of real estate investing and can provide invaluable insights.

6. Stay Disciplined with Your Finances

Maintaining financial discipline is key to long-term success in real estate. Ensure that you're managing your cash flow, avoiding overleveraging, and reinvesting profits strategically. Consistent and responsible financial management will provide the foundation for sustained growth.

How to Manage Finances:

Track your income and expenses to ensure positive cash flow.

Reinvest profits into new opportunities rather than using them for personal expenses.

7. Maintain a Positive Mindset

Staying motivated often comes down to your mindset. Real estate investing can be challenging, but maintaining a positive attitude and believing in your ability to succeed will keep you moving forward, even during tough times.

How to Cultivate Positivity:

Practice gratitude for your progress, no matter how small.

Focus on what you can control and let go of what you can't.

Stay motivated by visualizing the lifestyle and financial freedom your investments can bring.

8. Celebrate Your Progress

While the journey of real estate investing is ongoing, it's important to take time to celebrate your progress. Recognize your achievements, whether it's purchasing your first property or achieving a specific financial goal. Celebrating success boosts morale and fuels further progress.

How to Celebrate:

Acknowledge milestones and reward yourself for reaching them.

Take time to reflect on how far you've come and how much you've learned along the way.

9. Don't Lose Sight of Your "Why"

Your motivation will be strongest when you remember why you started in real estate investing in the first place. Whether it's to build long-term wealth, achieve financial independence, or secure a better future for your family, keep your "why" at the forefront of your mind.

How to Reconnect with Your Purpose:

Write down your reasons for investing and revisit them regularly.

Use your "why" as a source of motivation to keep pushing forward, especially when facing challenges.

Real estate investing is a rewarding yet demanding journey. To succeed in this field, you need a clear strategy, patience, and the ability to adapt as you learn and grow. Stay motivated by focusing on your goals, continuing to educate yourself, and surrounding yourself with a supportive network. As long as you remain committed and disciplined, your real estate investment journey will bring the financial rewards you seek.

Conclusion

By now, you should have a solid foundation in real estate investing. The knowledge you've gained throughout this book will serve as your roadmap, guiding you through each step of your investment journey. From understanding market cycles to managing your properties effectively, you now have the tools needed to make informed decisions and execute your first deal with confidence.

Real estate investing is a rewarding but long-term commitment. It requires patience, ongoing research, and continuous learning to stay ahead of market trends and maximize your returns. As you move forward, remember that each investment you make will bring new lessons, whether it's a success or a challenge.

As you grow your portfolio, don't forget the key principles that will guide you: sound financial management, thorough due diligence, and a disciplined approach to risk. Stay focused on your goals and adapt your strategies as you evolve as an investor.

Ultimately, the path to success in real estate investing is built on persistence, resilience, and the ability to learn from every experience. Keep moving forward, and with time and effort, you will see the rewards of your hard work. Happy investing!

Ending Notes

Congratulations on reaching the end of this journey! If you're holding this book in your hands, you're one step closer to transforming your future through real estate investing. It's not just about acquiring properties—it's about unlocking the potential to build wealth, create financial freedom, and leave a legacy. And you now have the knowledge to get started.

But here's the thing: this is just the beginning. The world of real estate is vast, and there's so much more to explore and learn. I hope the insights you've gained here are just the start of your ongoing education. The best investors are lifelong learners, continuously refining their skills, understanding market shifts, and adapting to new strategies. Stay curious. Keep asking questions. Don't be afraid to challenge your own assumptions. The more you learn, the more confident you'll become in making decisions that will move you toward your goals.

Real estate investing isn't always a straight path. It comes with its ups and downs, challenges and rewards. But each experience is a lesson that will prepare you for the next big

ENDING NOTES

opportunity. Just remember that patience and perseverance are key. Rome wasn't built in a day, and neither will your real estate empire. Take your time, make informed decisions, and don't rush the process.

Your first deal will be a milestone you'll never forget, and after that, it's all about growing and scaling. And when you face obstacles, remind yourself that every successful investor has been where you are right now—starting with nothing but knowledge and the drive to succeed.

I'm genuinely excited for you. You've taken the first steps to building something incredible. Stay focused, stay driven, and most importantly—stay inspired. There will be challenges, but if you keep your eyes on your goals and continue learning, there's no limit to what you can achieve. Here's to your success and to the journey ahead. You've got this!

Thank you for trusting me to guide you through this exciting chapter of your life. I can't wait to hear about your successes. Best of luck!

www.ingramcontent.com/pod-product-compliance
Lightning Source LLC
Chambersburg PA
CBHW071024240526
45469CB00006BD/2071